Point-of-Purchase

DESIGN ANNUAL

9

THE 44th MERCHANDISING AWARDS

VISUAL REFERENCE PUBLICATIONS, INC. / NEW YORK

Visual Reference Publications, Inc.
302 Fifth Avenue
New York, NY 10001

Distributors to the trade in the United States and Canada
Watson-Guptill
770 Broadway
New York, NY 10003

Distributors outside the United States and Canada
HarperCollins International
10 East 53rd Street
New York, NY 10022-5299

Library of Congress Cataloging in Publication Data:
Main entry under title: Point-of-Purchase Design Annual No. 9

Printed in China
ISBN 1-58471-065-9

Book design and type formatting by Bernard Schleifer

Contents

The POPAI Mission

POPAI is the international trade association of the point-of-purchase advertising industry, with more than half of its corporate affiliate members based outside the United States. POPAI is pursuing attainment of five operating goals emanating from its strategic plan:

1) establish P-O-P advertising a measured medium, on par with broadcast, print and other measured ad media;

2) capitalize on the increased use of technology to exploit unprecedented opportunities for an expanded role for in-store advertising;

3) address members' changing needs as business becomes more global;

4) be more inclusive of those engaged in activities relevant to P-O-P advertising;

5) enjoy a business environment characterized by ethical business practices, expanded opportunities and preservation of rights as an advertising medium.

Introduction

WHAT ARE THE POPAI OMA AWARDS?

POPAI's Outstanding Merchandising Achievement (OMA) Awards recognize excellence in in-store advertising. Entries are judged by a blue-ribbon panel of clients, based on the display's ability to increase sales, obtain retail placements, and work strategically to position the brand at the point of sale. For over forty years, POPAI's OMA Awards have recognized some of the most effective and original displays that industry has to offer, and is the premier awards recognition contest in the P-O-P advertising industry.

Teams of judges review images and case histories of the entries in each category, while also viewing the actual entries on the POP Marketplace show floor. The teams of judges then assign scores that will determine the winners.

POPAI's OMA Award winners receive statuettes, which are gold, silver, and bronze replicas of wooden cigar store Indians that once decorated the entrance of tobacco stores in the early Nineteenth Century. Carved by sailors from salvaged pieces of spars or masts from ships, these wooden figures are America's first known use of in-store advertising. Today, POPAI's OMA Awards statuette serves as a symbol of in-store advertising's evolution from this modest beginning as a reminder of the intimate connection between in-store advertising and consumer products.

POPAI's OMA Awards Contest is comprised of four contests:

1. **OMA Contest:** recognizes the excellence of entries produced and placed anywhere in the world.

2. **Multinational Contest:** recognizes the excellence of entries produced and placed only outside of the United States, Europe and Japan.

3. **Technical Contest:** recognizes engineering excellence, innovative qualities or a unique solution to a design challenge.

4. **Display of the Year Contest:** recognizes the best in P-O-P advertising from the three previous mentioned categories. A prestigious Display-of-the-Year (DOY) Award is bestowed upon one gold winner in each of the following: Permanent OMA, Semi-Permanent OMA, Temporary OMA, and Multinational Contest.

Merchandising Awards Judges

OMA Contest Judges

Ms. Carolyn Anderson
Dr. Pepper/Seven Up

Ms. Shelia Anderson
Mattel Toys Inc.

Mr. Paul Aspesi
Golden Books Family Entertainment

Mr. Steve Bartolucci
Sanford North America

Ms. Susan Bell
Keebler Company

Mr. Matt Borgard
Barton Beers Ltd.

Mr. Ted Brueggemann
Miller Brewing Company

Ms. Nancy Bruner
Kraft Foods

Mr. Jerry Cahee
Dicksons, Inc.

Mr. Greg Casey
Nintendo of America, Inc.

Ms. Suenhee Choi
Coty Beauty US

Ms. Penny Cleare
QP Group

Ms. Mary DaRif
Sherwin Williams

Mr. John Devine
Bose Corporation

Ms. Jennifer Dinehart
Corn Products International

Ms. Debbie Doerr
Wm. Wrigley Company

Ms. Bea Dorsey
Cooper Lighting

Mr. Ronald Elowitz
Schering-Plough Corporation

Ms. Linda Feldman
ICI Paints

Ms. Sandra M. Gallo
Miller Brewing Company

Ms. Kathleen Gaskill
E & J Gallo Winery

Mr. Scott Greenberg
Skechers USA

Mr. Michael Harris
Nabisco

Mr. Jay Hawkinson
The Dial Corporation

Mr. Stanley Jungenberg
Otis Spunkmeyer, Inc.

Mr. Stephen Kamp
Dr. Pepper/Seven Up

Ms. Lori Kirk-Rolley
Daltile Corp

Mr. Richard Kirwin
Snap-On Tools

Mr. Dennis Knaus
Diversified Merchandising Inc.

Mr. Kevin Kramnic
Barton Beers Ltd.

Mr. Michael Lopez
Kmart Corparation

Ms. Andrea Martin
E & J Gallo Winery

Ms. Teresa May
Procter & Gamble

Ms. Rosemary McDaniel
Bayer Corporation

Ms. Tina Petro
McCormick & Company

Ms. Renee Ray
Procter & Gamble

Mr. Joe Sadtler
M&M/Mars

Mr. John Sakaley
Nintendo of America, Inc.

Ms. Jeanie Swanson
Jim Beam Brands Co.

Ms. Laura Van Haaren
Microsoft

Mr. Dan Vnencak
Nabisco

Mr. Kurt Witzel
Anheuser-Busch Inc.

Mr. Gary Young
General Motors Corporation

Multinational Contest Judges

Mr. Bill Alexiou
Coca-Cola South Pacific

Mr. Martin John Alford
Total Fima Elf

Mr. Stephen De Lorenzo
POP Productions

Ms Rita Eriksson
Shoppers Drug Mart

Mr. Oscar Norbeto
Marcovecchio Stopromotion Group

Mr. Hector Luis Mendoza Lavin
Unilever de Mexico HPC

Ms. Lisa Oversby
Cheltenham & Gloucester PLC

Technical Contest Judges

Mr. Bill Abene
Panel Prints Inc.

Mr. Daniel Berneche
Promoflex International

Mr. Herm Buechel
Ivex Packaging Corp.

Mr. David Censi
Mystic Display Co.

Mr. Mark Dillon
Meyers Display

Mr. Joe Fish
Hankscraft Motors, Inc.

Mr. David Foster
E & E Display

Mr. Jody Libman
Terrace Display Group

Mr. David May
Lingo Manufacturing Company, Inc.

Mr. Kevin Saladyga
Packaging Specialists

Mr. James Shinker
Madden Communications

Mr. Fred Sklenar
Abstrategy Design

Mr. Mark Stanton
Tri-Star Plastics LLC

Display of the Year Judges

Ms. Shelia Anderson
Mattel Toys

Mr. Steve Bartolucci
Samford North America

Mr. Ted Brueggemann
Miller Brewing Company

Ms. Nancy Bruner
Kraft Foods

Mr. Jerry Cahee
Dicksons, Inc.

Mr. Greg Casey
Nintendo of America Inc.

Ms. Penny Cleare
QP Group

Ms. Sandra Gallo
Miller Brewing Company

Mr. Jay Hawkinson
The Dial Corporation

Mr. Richard Kirwin
Snap-On Tools

Mr. Michael Lanaghan
Wm. Wrigley Jr. Company

Ms. Andrea Martin
E & J Gallo Winery

Mr. Joe Sadtler
M&M/Mars

Mr. John Sakaley
Nintendo of America, Inc.

Display of the Year Contest Winners

Display of the Year Winners

TITLE
LeapFrog Interactive Kiosk

CLIENT
LeapFrog

ENTRANT
Design Phase, Inc.
Northbrook, Illinois

SUB-CATEGORY
Toys

DIVISION
Permanent

OBJECTIVES
Create larger than life Interactive Kiosk, capture brand identity through design, color, quality, characters and trust of the LeapFrog brand.

MATERIALS
Vacuum Form characters, logo, monitor shroud, monitor cover and body. Internal wood structure. Sheet Metal to secure parts. 4 color Graphics.
PLASTIC PARTS: 3 Frog Header—pre-printed 4-color process, Logo Header, Monitor Shroud, Drawer Cover, 3 part display body. All parts vacuum formed and routed to size. WOOD: Internal wood structure supporting display bottom interior and a wood spine. SHEET METAL: Approximately 17 different steel brackets and formed parts, including "L" brackets, secure monitor and assemble parts, and steel drawer and monitor stand. GRAPHICS: 4-color process on pressure sensitive styrene and 10-point white tag stock. 10 different decals total.

SEMI-PERMANENT DISPLAY OF THE YEAR WINNER

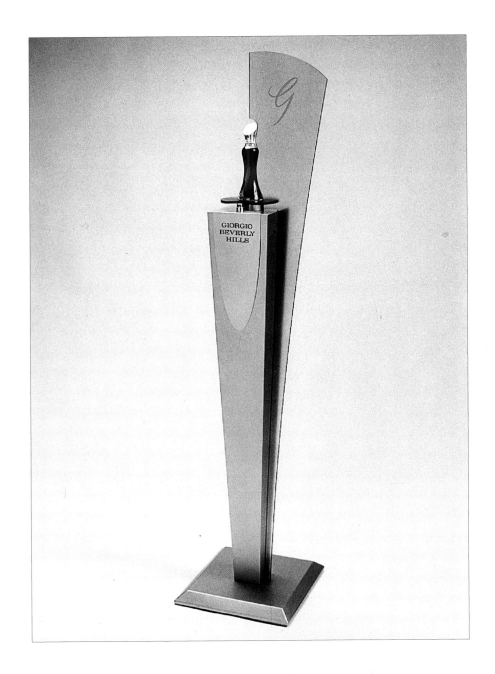

TITLE
Giorgio Beverly Hills "G" Displays

CLIENT
Procter & Gamble Prestige Beauté

ENTRANT
Diam International Ltd.
Loughborough, Leicestershire, United Kingdom

SUB-CATEGORY
Women's Perfumes

DIVISION
Semi-Permanent

OBJECTIVES
To promote and provide a tester vehicle for "G" fragrances in harmony with brand equity.

MATERIALS
MDF, injection moulded acrylic, steel, plastic fabrication, paint spraying

MDF, Injection Molded Acrylic, Sheet Steel, Plastic Fabrication"

TEMPORARY DISPLAY OF THE YEAR WINNER

TITLE
Olay "Visionary Light" Color Promotion

CLIENT
Procter & Gamble Cosmetics

ENTRANT
Rock-Tenn Company Alliance Group
Hunt Valley, Maryland

SUB-CATEGORY
Multiple Product Line Merchandising

DIVISION
Temporary

OBJECTIVES
Continue to establish Olay as an authority in color by delivering colors on trend, updating & bonding w/women by offering colors that free their inner glow.

MATERIALS
Thermaform & injection molded transluscent trays, shade labels, 6 color offset 10 pt SBS laminated to E flute corrugated.

Injection Molded ABS main structure tinted purple, Thermaform tray opaque pearl with purple flake, shade labels flexo printed with multiple shade matches for lip colors. Headers are 6 color offset printed on 10 pt SBS singleface laminated to E flute corrugated.

MULTINATIONAL DISPLAY OF THE YEAR WINNER

TITLE
Cappuccino Self Standing Display

CLIENT
Nestlé México, S.A. de C.V.

ENTRANT
Armo Diseno, POP, S.C.
Mexico DF, Mexico

SUB-CATEGORY
Multinational Contest

DIVISION
Semi-Permanent

OBJECTIVES
Support the introductory phase of a new line of coffee products and communicate their benefits.

MATERIALS
Wire structure with Vacuum formed poli stirene header, footer and shelves.
Side graphics printed in silk screen four color process over poli styrene

POPAI's Outstanding Merchandising Achievement (OMA) Awards Contest

The OMA Contest recognizes merchandising excellence of displays produced and placed anywhere in the world.

AWARD
Gold

TITLE
Budweiser Bud One Motion Sign

CLIENT
Anheuser-Busch, Inc.

ENTRANT
Everbrite, Inc.
Greenfield, Wisconsin

SUB-CATEGORY
On-Premise – Illuminated or Motion

DIVISION
Permanent

AWARD
Gold

TITLE
Budweiser/Nascar Motion Sign

CLIENT
Anheuser-Busch, Inc.

ENTRANT
Gage In-Store Marketing
Minneapolis, Minnesota

SUB-CATEGORY
Off-Premise – Illuminated or Motion

DIVISION
Permanent

Beverages—Beer

AWARD
Silver

TITLE
Busch Nascar Auto Hood

CLIENT
Anheuser-Busch, Inc.

ENTRANT
Grimm Industries Inc.
Fairview, Pennsylvania

SUB-CATEGORY
On-Premise – Non-Illuminated
or Non-Motion

DIVISION
Permanent

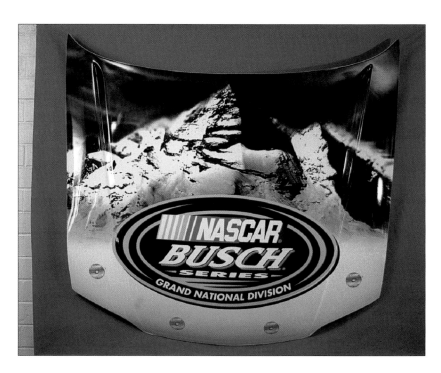

AWARD
Silver

TITLE
Busch Bass 3-D Wall Sign

CLIENT
Anheuser-Busch, Inc.

ENTRANT
Moldrite Products, Inc.
Waukesha, Wisconsin

SUB-CATEGORY
On-Premise – Non-Illuminated or Non-Motion

DIVISION
Permanent

AWARD
Silver

TITLE
Leinenkugel's Muskie Wall Clock

CLIENT
Miller Brewing Company

ENTRANT
Moldrite Products, Inc.
Waukesha, Wisconsin

SUB-CATEGORY
On-Premise – Illuminated or Motion

DIVISION
Permanent

AWARD
Silver

TITLE
Icehouse Neon Spectacular Sign

CLIENT
Miller Brewing Company

ENTRANT
Moldrite Products, Inc. and Fallon
Waukesha, Wisconsin

SUB-CATEGORY
On-Premise – Illuminated or Motion

DIVISION
Permanent

AWARD
Bronze

TITLE
Budweiser Classic Script Neon
Sign Program

CLIENT
Anheuser-Busch, Inc.

ENTRANT
Everbrite, Inc.
Greenfield, Wisconsin

SUB-CATEGORY
Off-Premise – Illuminated or Motion

DIVISION
Permanent

AWARD
Bronze

TITLE
Miller High Life Art Deco Neon

CLIENT
Miller Brewing Company

ENTRANT
Fallon Luminous Products Corporation
Spartanburg, South Carolina

SUB-CATEGORY
On-Premise – Illuminated or Motion

DIVISION
Permanent

AWARD
Bronze

TITLE
Coors Light Texas Proud Neon

CLIENT
The Integer Group

ENTRANT
Fallon Luminous Products Corporation
Spartanburg, South Carolina

SUB-CATEGORY
On-Premise – Illuminated or Motion

DIVISION
Permanent

AWARD
Bronze

TITLE
Budweiser Backlit Sign

CLIENT
Anheuser-Busch, Inc.

ENTRANT
Grimm Industries Inc.
Fairview, Pennsylvania

SUB-CATEGORY
On-Premise – Non-Illuminated or
Non-Motion

DIVISION
Permanent

AWARD
Bronze

TITLE
Illuminated Labatt Bottle Menu Board

CLIENT
The Alison Group

ENTRANT
Grimm Industries Inc.
Fairview, Pennsylvania

SUB-CATEGORY
On-Premise – Illuminated or Motion

DIVISION
Permanent

AWARD
Silver

TITLE
Budweiser Clydesdale
Half Wagon

CLIENT
Anheuser-Busch, Inc.

ENTRANT
Anheuser-Busch, Inc.
St. Louis, Missouri

SUB-CATEGORY
Off-Premise –
Non-Illuminated or
Non-Motion

DIVISION
Semi-Permanent

AWARD
Bronze

TITLE
Pabst Brewing Company
Metal Tacker Program

CLIENT
Pabst Brewing Company

ENTRANT
Bish Creative Display Inc.
Lake Zurich, Illinois

SUB-CATEGORY
On-Premise – Non-Illuminated
or Non-Motion

DIVISION
Semi-Permanent

AWARD
Bronze

TITLE
Longneck Bottle Iceman

CLIENT
Miller Brewing Company

ENTRANT
Paul Flum Ideas, Inc.
St. Louis, Missouri

SUB-CATEGORY
On-Premise –
Non-Illuminated or
Non-Motion

DIVISION
Semi-Permanent

AWARD
Gold

TITLE
Budweiser Hacienda Case Stacker

CLIENT
Anheuser-Busch, Inc.

ENTRANT
Rapid Displays
Union City, California

SUB-CATEGORY
Off-Premise – Non-Illuminated
or Non-Motion

DIVISION
Temporary

AWARD
Silver

TITLE
Tequiza Pinata

CLIENT
Anheuser-Busch, Inc.

ENTRANT
Anheuser-Busch, Inc.
St. Louis, Missouri

SUB-CATEGORY
Off-Premise – Non-Illuminated
or Non-Motion

DIVISION
Temporary

AWARD
Bronze

TITLE
Lysholmer Beer Display

CLIENT
Ringnes AS Trade Marketing

ENTRANT
Leo Burnett Oslo
Oslo, Norway

SUB-CATEGORY
Off-Premise – Non-Illuminated
or Non-Motion

DIVISION
Temporary

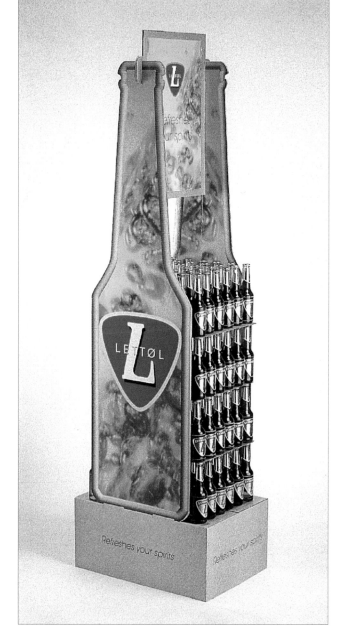

AWARD
Bronze

TITLE
Michelob Fireplace

CLIENT
Anheuser-Busch, Inc

ENTRANT
Phoenix Display/International Paper
Thorofare, New Jersey

SUB-CATEGORY
Off-Premise – Non-Illuminated or Non-Motion

DIVISION
Temporary

Beverages—Liquor

AWARD
Gold

TITLE
Dewars Acrylic Two Case Merchandiser

CLIENT
Bacardi Martini

ENTRANT
Bish Creative Display Inc.
Lake Zurich, Illinois

SUB-CATEGORY
Distilled Spirits – Non-Illuminated or
Non-Motion

DIVISION
Permanent

AWARD
Gold

TITLE
Hot Damn Fire Extinguisher

CLIENT
Jim Beam Brands Company

ENTRANT
Bish Creative Display Inc.
Lake Zurich, Illinois

SUB-CATEGORY
Distilled Spirits – Illuminated or Motion

DIVISION
Permanent

AWARD
Silver

TITLE
Jim Beam Pool Table Mass Display

CLIENT
Jim Beam Brands Company

ENTRANT
Bish Creative Display Inc.
Lake Zurich, Illinois

SUB-CATEGORY
Distilled Spirits – Non-Illuminated
or Non-Motion

DIVISION
Permanent

AWARD
Silver

TITLE
Quality Wines Floor Display

CLIENT
SAQ Alimentation

ENTRANT
Point 1 Displays Inc.
Montreal, Quebec, Canada

SUB-CATEGORY
Cordial and Wines

DIVISION
Permanent

Beverages—Liquor

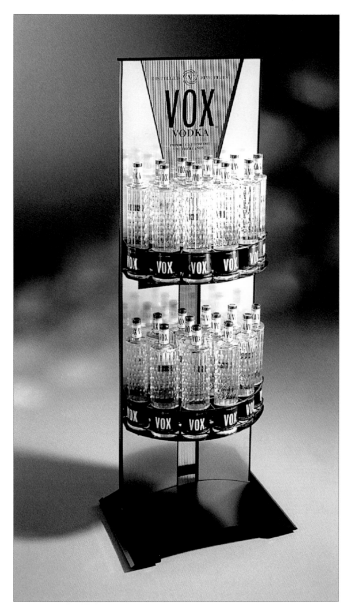

AWARD
Silver

TITLE
Jim Beam Vox Vodka Floor Display

CLIENT
Jim Beam Brands

ENTRANT
The Niven Marketing Group
Bensenville, Illinois

SUB-CATEGORY
Distilled Spirits – Non-Illuminated or
Non-Motion

DIVISION
Permanent

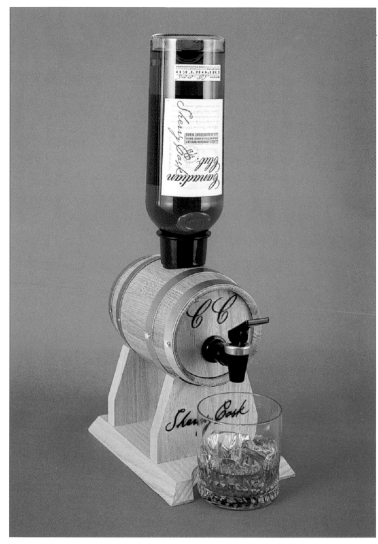

AWARD
Bronze

TITLE
Canadian Club Sherry Cask

CLIENT
Allied Domecq

ENTRANT
Bish Creative Display Inc.
Lake Zurich, Illinois

SUB-CATEGORY
Distilled Spirits – Non-Illuminated or Non-
Motion

DIVISION
Permanent

AWARD
Bronze

TITLE
Windsor Canadian Stadium Mass Display

CLIENT
Jim Beam Brands Company

ENTRANT
Bish Creative Display Inc.
Lake Zurich, Illinois

SUB-CATEGORY
Distilled Spirits – Non-Illuminated or Non-Motion

DIVISION
Permanent

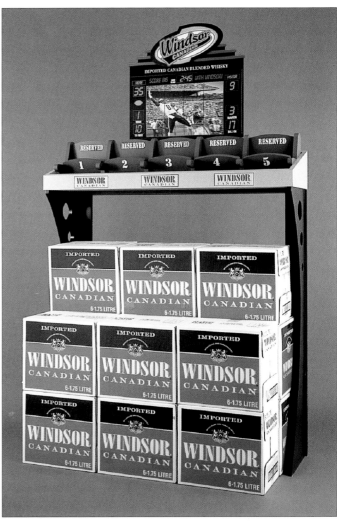

AWARD
Bronze

TITLE
Jose Cuervo Modular Display

CLIENT
UDV, Southwest

ENTRANT
Flair Display, Inc.
Bronx, New York

SUB-CATEGORY
Distilled Spirits – Illuminated
or Motion

DIVISION
Permanent

Beverages—Liquor

AWARD
Bronze

TITLE
Evan Williams Kentucky Bourbon
Floor Display

CLIENT
Heaven Hill Distilleries, Inc.

ENTRANT
Flair Display, Inc.
Bronx, New York

SUB-CATEGORY
Distilled Spirits – Non-Illuminated or
Non-Motion

DIVISION
Permanent

AWARD
Bronze

TITLE
BRL Hardy Wine Display

CLIENT
BRL Hardy Wine Company

ENTRANT
Visy Displays
(A Division of Pratt Industries)
Reservoir, Victoria, Australia

SUB-CATEGORY
Cordial and Wines

DIVISION
Permanent

AWARD
Bronze

TITLE
E & J Gallo Wild Vines Bottle

CLIENT
E & J Gallo Winery

ENTRANT
Joliet Pattern, Inc.
Crest Hill, Illinois

SUB-CATEGORY
Cordial and Wines

DIVISION
Permanent

AWARD
Gold

TITLE
Haywood New Package
Relaunch Program

CLIENT
Haywood Winery

ENTRANT
Rack's Inc.
San Diego, California

SUB-CATEGORY
Cordial and Wines

DIVISION
Semi-Permanent

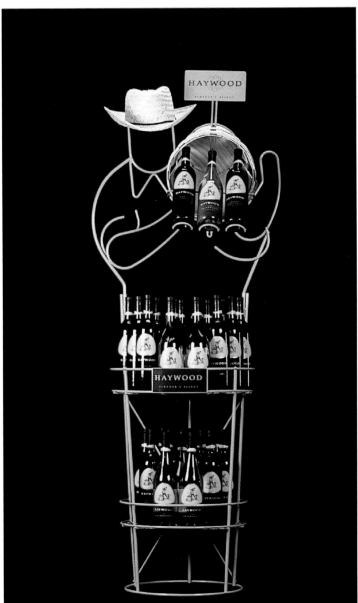

AWARD
Silver

TITLE
E & J Brandy 25th Anniversary
Floor Display

CLIENT
E & J Gallo Winery

ENTRANT
Rack's Inc. and Bert-Co Graphics
San Diego, California

SUB-CATEGORY
Cordial and Wines

DIVISION
Semi-Permanent

AWARD
Silver

TITLE
Absolut Jackpot Mass Display

CLIENT
Seagram Americas

ENTRANT
Upshot
Chicago, Illinois

SUB-CATEGORY
Distilled Spirits – Illuminated
or Motion

DIVISION
Semi-Permanent

AWARD
Bronze

TITLE
Tanqueray No. Ten Floor Display

CLIENT
Schieffelin & Somerset

ENTRANT
Flair Display, Inc.
Bronx, New York

SUB-CATEGORY
Distilled Spirits – Non-Illuminated
or Non-Motion

DIVISION
Semi-Permanent

AWARD
Bronze

TITLE
Absolut Mandarin Floor Rack

CLIENT
Seagram Americas

ENTRANT
Display Products N.A. Inc.
Yaphank, New York

SUB-CATEGORY
Distilled Spirits – Non-Illuminated
or Non-Motion

DIVISION
Semi-Permanent

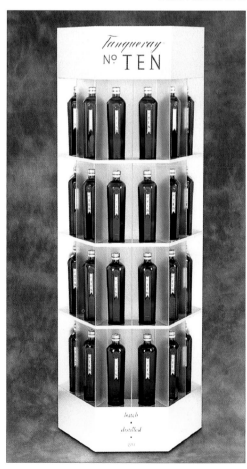

AWARD
Gold

TITLE
Canadian Club Holiday Program

CLIENT
Allied Domecq

ENTRANT
Bish Creative Display Inc.
Lake Zurich, Illinois

SUB-CATEGORY
Distilled Spirits – Non-Illuminated or
Non-Motion

DIVISION
Temporary

AWARD
Gold

TITLE
Absolut Gift End Aisle Display

CLIENT
Seagram Americas

ENTRANT
Upshot
Chicago, Illinois

SUB-CATEGORY
Distilled Spirits – Illuminated
or Motion

DIVISION
Temporary

AWARD
Gold

TITLE
Absolut Spontaneity
End Aisle Display

CLIENT
Seagram Americas

ENTRANT
Upshot
Chicago, Illinois

SUB-CATEGORY
Distilled Spirits – Non-Illuminated
or Non-Motion

DIVISION
Temporary

AWARD
Silver

TITLE
Bacardi Summer Rhumba Pole Display

CLIENT
Bacardi Martini

ENTRANT
Bish Creative Display Inc.
Lake Zurich, Illinois

SUB-CATEGORY
Distilled Spirits – Non-Illuminated
or Non-Motion

DIVISION
Temporary

AWARD
Silver

TITLE
Remy Red Floorstand

CLIENT
Remy Amerique, Inc.

ENTRANT
MBH Presentations, Inc.
Floral Park, New York

SUB-CATEGORY
Distilled Spirits – Non-Illuminated
or Non-Motion

DIVISION
Temporary

AWARD
Silver

TITLE
Absolut Attraction End Aisle Display

CLIENT
Seagram Americas

ENTRANT
Upshot
Chicago, Illinois

SUB-CATEGORY
Distilled Spirits – Illuminated or Motion

DIVISION
Temporary

AWARD
Bronze

TITLE
Seagram's 'Absolut' Case Backer

CLIENT
Joseph E. Seagram & Sons, Limited

ENTRANT
Artisan Display, Ltd.
Markham, Ontario, Canada

SUB-CATEGORY
Distilled Spirits – Non-Illuminated
or Non-Motion

DIVISION
Temporary

AWARD
Bronze

TITLE
Jack Daniel's Holiday 2000 Display

CLIENT
DraftWorldwide for Brown Forman

ENTRANT
Rapid Displays
Union City, California

SUB-CATEGORY
Distilled Spirits – Illuminated or Motion

DIVISION
Temporary

AWARD
Bronze

TITLE
Jack Daniel's Holiday Case Card

CLIENT
DraftWorldwide for Brown Forman

ENTRANT
Rapid Displays
Chicago, Illinois

SUB-CATEGORY
Distilled Spirits – Non-Illuminated
or Non-Motion

DIVISION
Temporary

AWARD
Bronze

TITLE
Crown Royal Holiday Motion Display

CLIENT
DCS Marketing/Upshot/Seagrams

ENTRANT
Rapid Displays
Chicago, Illinois

SUB-CATEGORY
Distilled Spirits – Illuminated or Motion

DIVISION
Temporary

AWARD
Bronze

TITLE
Dekuyper Holiday 2000 "Disco" Display

CLIENT
Jim Beam Brands Company

ENTRANT
Rapid Displays
Chicago, Illinois

SUB-CATEGORY
Distilled Spirits – Illuminated or Motion

DIVISION
Temporary

AWARD
Bronze

TITLE
Smirnoff Holiday Wreath Display

CLIENT
United Distillers and Vitners

ENTRANT
Rapid Displays
Chicago, Illinois

SUB-CATEGORY
Distilled Spirits – Illuminated or Motion

DIVISION
Temporary

AWARD
Bronze

TITLE
Oregon Lottery Keno Motion Clock

CLIENT
Oregon Lottery

ENTRANT
Heritage Sign & Display, Inc.
Nesquehoning, Pennsylvania

SUB-CATEGORY
Convenient Store Retailer
(Traditional/Petroleum, w/wo gas)

DIVISION
Permanent

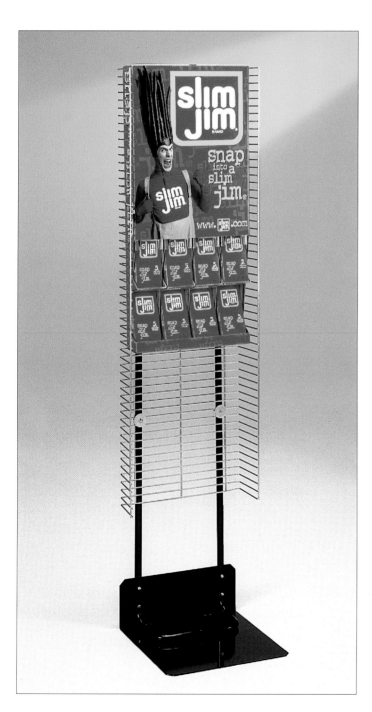

AWARD
Bronze

TITLE
Goodmark Slim Jim Handi Pak Powerwing

CLIENT
Goodmark Foods, Inc.

ENTRANT
Triangle Display Group
Philadelphia, Pennsylvania

SUB-CATEGORY
Convenient Store Retailer
(Traditional/Petroleum, w/wo gas)

DIVISION
Temporary

AWARD
Gold

TITLE
Hard Candy Counter Display and Floor Stand

CLIENT
Hard Candy

ENTRANT
The Royal Promotion Group Inc.
New York, New York

SUB-CATEGORY
Multiple Product Line Merchandising

DIVISION
Permanent

AWARD
Silver

TITLE
Calvin Klein Cosmetics
Seasonal Tester Unit

CLIENT
Unilever Cosmetics International

ENTRANT
Consumer Promotions International
Mount Vernon, New York

SUB-CATEGORY
Testers

DIVISION
Permanent

AWARD
Silver

TITLE
Tony & Tina Full Line Display

CLIENT
Tony & Tina Cosmetics

ENTRANT
The Royal Promotion Group Inc.
New York, New York

SUB-CATEGORY
Multiple Product Line
Merchandising

DIVISION
Permanent

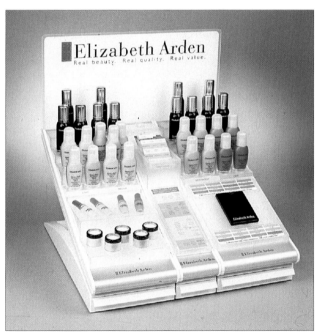

AWARD
Bronze

TITLE
The Elizabeth Arden Foundation Display

CLIENT
Elizabeth Arden Company

ENTRANT
Consumer Promotions International
Mount Vernon, New York

SUB-CATEGORY
Single Product Line Merchandising

DIVISION
Permanent

AWARD
Bronze

TITLE
Chanel Color Playstation

CLIENT
Chanel

ENTRANT
Consumer Promotions International
Mount Vernon, New York

SUB-CATEGORY
Multiple Product Line Merchandising

DIVISION
Permanent

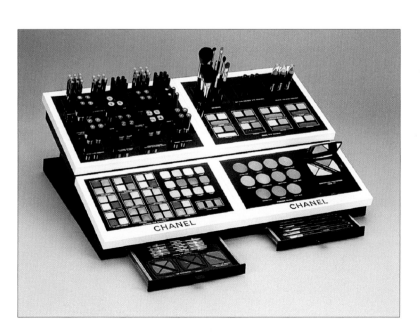

Cosmetics—Women

AWARD
Bronze

TITLE
Make-Up General Tester Unit By Lancôme

CLIENT
Lancôme

CLIENT
Lancôme International

ENTRANT
Diam Group
Les Mureaux, France

SUB-CATEGORY
Testers

DIVISION
Permanent

AWARD
Bronze

TITLE
Bobbi Brown Master Essentials Tester

CLIENT
Bobbi Brown Professional Cosmetics

ENTRANT
The Royal Promotion Group Inc.
New York, New York

SUB-CATEGORY
Multiple Product Line Merchandising

DIVISION
Permanent

AWARD
Gold

TITLE
Cover Girl Smoothers

CLIENT
Procter & Gamble

ENTRANT
Array Marketing Group
/IDMD Design & Manufacturing, Inc.
Toronto, Ontario, Canada

SUB-CATEGORY
Multiple Product Line Merchandising

DIVISION
Semi-Permanent

AWARD
Gold

TITLE
Olay "What's New" Complete Radiance Launch

CLIENT
Procter & Gamble Cosmetics

ENTRANT
Rock-Tenn Company Alliance Group
Hunt Valley, Maryland

SUB-CATEGORY
Multiple Product Line Merchandising

DIVISION
Semi-Permanent

AWARD
Gold

TITLE
Maybelline New Foundation Air Talker

CLIENT
Maybelline

ENTRANT
Ultimate Display Industries Inc.
Jamaica, New York

SUB-CATEGORY
Single Product Line Merchandising

DIVISION
Semi-Permanent

AWARD
Silver

TITLE
Estée Lauder "Go Pout" Tester Display

CLIENT
Estée Lauder, Inc.

ENTRANT
Consumer Promotions International
Mount Vernon, New York

SUB-CATEGORY
Single Product Line Merchandising

DIVISION
Semi-Permanent

AWARD
Silver

TITLE
Eye Catching Prescriptives

CLIENT
Estée Lauder Companies

ENTRANT
Triangle Display Group
Philadelphia, Pennsylvania

SUB-CATEGORY
Testers

DIVISION
Semi-Permanent

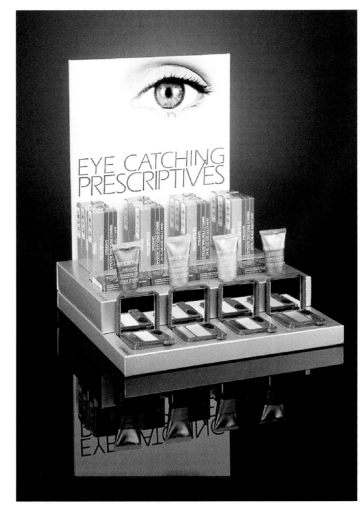

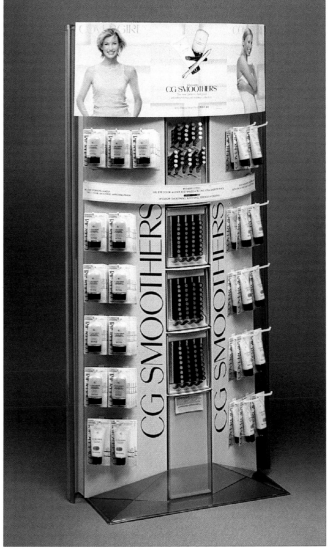

AWARD
Bronze

TITLE
Cover Girl Smoothers Floorstand/Endcap

CLIENT
Procter & Gamble Cosmetics

ENTRANT
Rock-Tenn Company Alliance Group
Hunt Valley, Maryland

SUB-CATEGORY
Multiple Product Line Merchandising

DIVISION
Semi-Permanent

Cosmetics—Women

AWARD
Bronze

TITLE
Wear 'N Go Launch Counter

CLIENT
Maybelline

ENTRANT
Ultimate Display Industries Inc.
Jamaica, New York

SUB-CATEGORY
Single Product Line Merchandising

DIVISION
Semi-Permanent

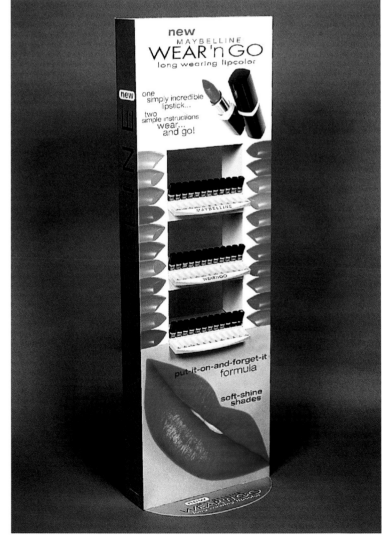

AWARD
Bronze

TITLE
Maybelline Wear 'N Go Launch Tower

CLIENT
Maybelline

ENTRANT
Ultimate Display Industries Inc.
Jamaica, New York

SUB-CATEGORY
Single Product Line Merchandising

DIVISION
Semi-Permanent

AWARD
Gold

TITLE
Olay "Visionary Light" Floorstand/Endcap

CLIENT
Procter & Gamble Cosmetics

ENTRANT
Rock-Tenn Company Alliance Group
Hunt Valley, Maryland

SUB-CATEGORY
Multiple Product Line Merchandising

DIVISION
Temporary

AWARD
Gold

TITLE
Olay "Visionary Light" Color Promotion

CLIENT
Procter & Gamble Cosmetics

ENTRANT
Rock-Tenn Company Alliance Group
Hunt Valley, Maryland

SUB-CATEGORY
Multiple Product Line Merchandising

DIVISION
Temporary

AWARD
Gold

TITLE
L'Oréal Colour Riche Wal-Mart Wedge

CLIENT
L'Oréal Canada

ENTRANT
Techno P.O.S. Inc.
Montreal, Quebec, Canada

SUB-CATEGORY
Multiple Product Line Merchandising

DIVISION
Temporary

AWARD
Silver

TITLE
L'Oréal Feather Counter Display

CLIENT
L'Oréal, Inc.

ENTRANT
Display Producers Inc.
Bronx, New York

SUB-CATEGORY
Single Product Line Merchandising

DIVISION
Temporary

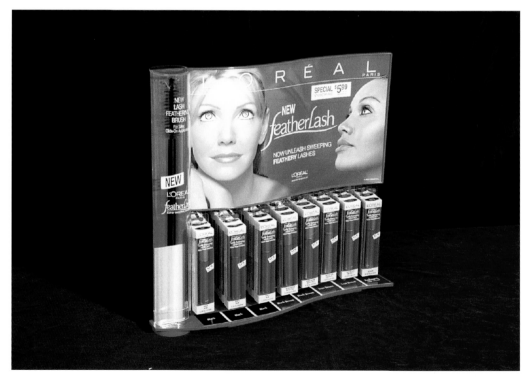

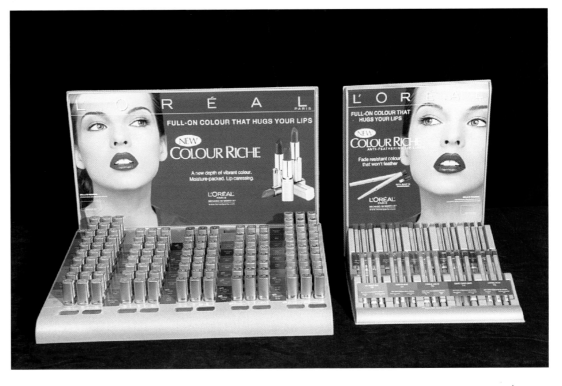

AWARD
Silver

TITLE
L'Oréal Colour Riche Lip Liner

CLIENT
L'Oréal, Inc.

ENTRANT
Display Producers Inc.
Bronx, New York

SUB-CATEGORY
Single Product Line Merchandising

DIVISION
Temporary

AWARD
Silver

TITLE
Bath and Body "Art Stuff" Sampling Kiosk

CLIENT
Bath and Body Works

ENTRANT
Rapid Displays
Chicago, Illinois

SUB-CATEGORY
Testers

DIVISION
Temporary

AWARD
Bronze

TITLE
L'Oréal Winter Shade Promotion

CLIENT
L'Oréal, Inc.

ENTRANT
Display Producers Inc.
Bronx, New York

SUB-CATEGORY
Single Product Line Merchandising

DIVISION
Temporary

AWARD
Bronze

TITLE
L'Oréal Winter Shade Nail

CLIENT
L'Oréal, Inc.

ENTRANT
Display Producers Inc.
Bronx, New York

SUB-CATEGORY
Single Product Line Merchandising

DIVISION
Temporary

AWARD
Bronze

TITLE
L'Oréal Winter Shade Eye Gloss

CLIENT
L'Oréal, Inc.

ENTRANT
Display Producers Inc.
Bronx, New York

SUB-CATEGORY
Single Product Line Merchandising

DIVISION
Temporary

AWARD
Bronze

TITLE
Maybelline Fall Animation Wal-Mart
Tower

CLIENT
L'Oréal Canada

ENTRANT
Techno P.O.S. Inc.
Montreal, Quebec, Canada

SUB-CATEGORY
Multiple Product Line Merchandising

DIVISION
Temporary

AWARD
Bronze

TITLE
L'Oréal FeatherLash Launch

CLIENT
L'Oréal Canada

ENTRANT
Techno P.O.S. Inc.
Montreal, Quebec, Canada

SUB-CATEGORY
Single Product Line Merchandising

DIVISION
Temporary

Drug Store Retailer

AWARD
Gold

TITLE
Duracell London Drugs 23" Spinner

CLIENT
Duracell

ENTRANT
New Dimensions Research Corp.
Melville, New York

SUB-CATEGORY
Drug Store Retailer
(Stand Alone/Strip Mall, Store Size)

DIVISION
Permanent

AWARD
Silver

TITLE
Tape/Kraft Paper/Envelope Floorstand
Display

CLIENT
Manco Inc.

ENTRANT
Packaging Corporation of America (PCA)
South Gate, California

SUB-CATEGORY
Drug Store Retailer
(Stand Alone/Strip Mall, Store Size)

DIVISION
Semi-Permanent

AWARD
Bronze

TITLE
Sundamentals Floor Display

CLIENT
Donegal Bay

ENTRANT
Pride Container/Display Graphics LLC
Chicago, Illinois

SUB-CATEGORY
Drug Store Retailer
(Stand Alone/Strip Mall, Store Size)

DIVISION
Semi-Permanent

AWARD
Bronze

TITLE
Silken Mist FS/PW

CLIENT
Sara Lee Hosiery

ENTRANT
Smurfit-Stone Display Group
Sandston, Virginia

SUB-CATEGORY
Drug Store Retailer
(Stand Alone/Strip Mall, Store Size)

DIVISION
Temporary

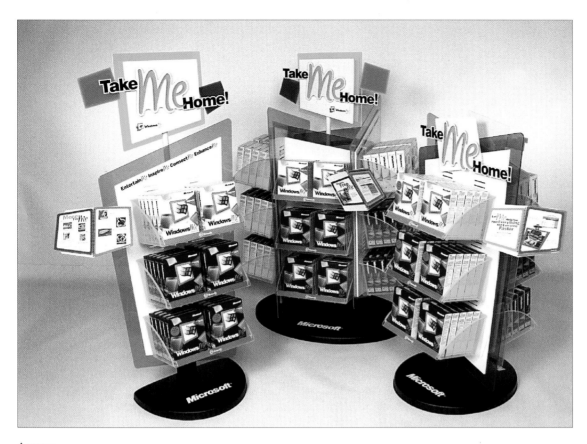

AWARD
Gold

TITLE
Display Program for Windows Millenium
Edition

CLIENT
Microsoft Corporation

ENTRANT
Design Phase, Inc.
Northbrook, Illinois

SUB-CATEGORY
Computer Software

DIVISION
Permanent

AWARD
Gold

TITLE
Microsoft MSN® Internet Center
for RadioShack

CLIENT
Microsoft Corporation

ENTRANT
HMG Schutz International Inc.
Morton Grove, Illinois

SUB-CATEGORY
Home Entertainment – Interactive,
Motion, or Illuminated

DIVISION
Permanent

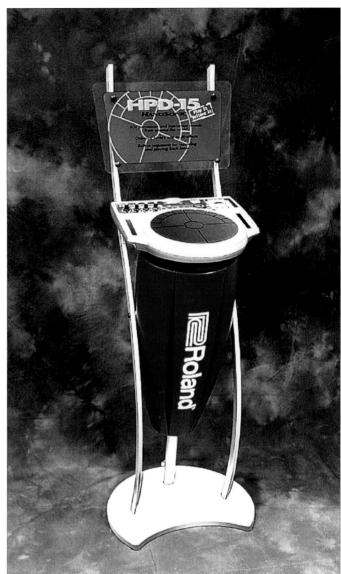

AWARD
Silver

TITLE
Roland HPD-15 Conga Drum Display

CLIENT
Roland Corporation

ENTRANT
Justman Packaging & Display
Los Angeles, California

SUB-CATEGORY
Home Entertainment – Interactive,
Motion, or Illuminated

DIVISION
Permanent

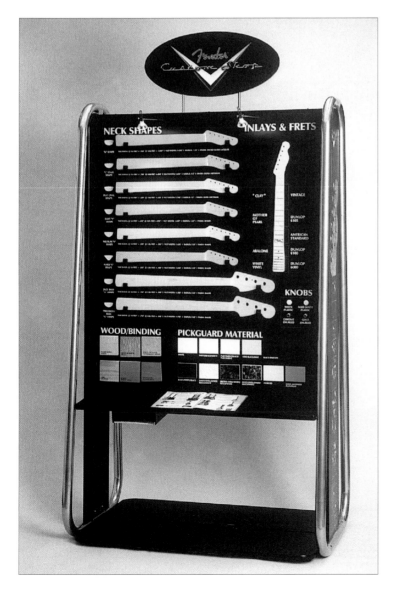

AWARD
Silver

TITLE
Fender Custom Shop

CLIENT
Fender Musical Instruments

ENTRANT
United Displaycraft
Des Plaines, Illinois

SUB-CATEGORY
Home Entertainment – Interactive,
Motion, or Illuminated

DIVISION
Permanent

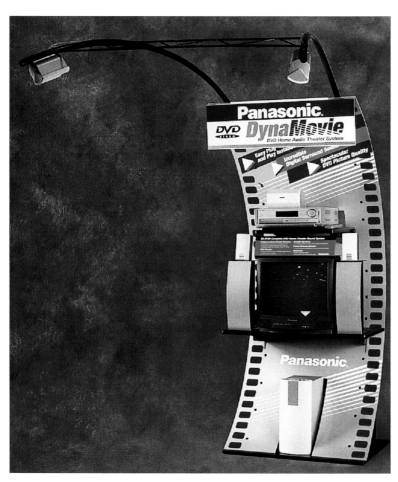

AWARD
Bronze

TITLE
Panasonic Home Theater Display

CLIENT
PCEC Communications, Panasonic

ENTRANT
Gage In-Store Marketing
Minneapolis, Minnesota

SUB-CATEGORY
Home Entertainment –
Non-Interactive, Non-Motion,
or Non-Illuminated

DIVISION
Permanent

AWARD
Bronze

TITLE
Panasonic Portable DVD Counter Display

CLIENT
PCEC Communications, Panasonic

ENTRANT
Gage In-Store Marketing
Minneapolis, Minnesota

SUB-CATEGORY
Home Entertainment – Non-Interactive,
Non-Motion, or Non-Illuminated

DIVISION
Permanent

AWARD
Bronze

TITLE
Sony Wega Floorstand

CLIENT
Sony

ENTRANT
The Display Connection
Moonachie, New Jersey

SUB-CATEGORY
Home Entertainment –
Non-Interactive, Non-Motion,
or Non-Illuminated

DIVISION
Permanent

AWARD
Bronze

TITLE
Xerox DisplayFlex/DemoFlash
Merchandiser

CLIENT
Xerox Corporation

ENTRANT
JPMS Inc.
Santa Fe Springs, California

SUB-CATEGORY
Computer Hardware

DIVISION
Permanent

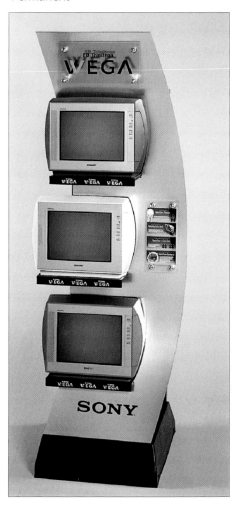

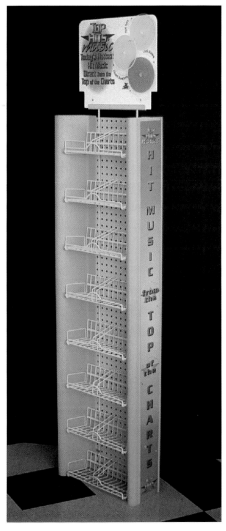

AWARD
Bronze

TITLE
Top Hits Power Wing

CLIENT
Top Hits Music

ENTRANT
Terrace Display Group
Cicero, Illinois

SUB-CATEGORY
Movies, Tapes, Records, CDs

DIVISION
Permanent

AWARD
Gold

TITLE
Disney 4th Quarter Destination

CLIENT
Buena Vista Home Entertainment

ENTRANT
Smurfit-Stone Display Group and
Cameo Container
Chicago, Illinois

SUB-CATEGORY
Movies, Tapes, Records, CDs

DIVISION
Semi-Permanent

AWARD
Silver

TITLE
Fox Home Entertainment Space Saver

CLIENT
Fox Home Entertainment

ENTRANT
Design Phase, Inc.
Northbrook, Illinois

SUB-CATEGORY
Movies, Tapes, Records, CDs

DIVISION
Semi-Permanent

AWARD
Silver

TITLE
Pentium IV Fall Launch

CLIENT
Intel Corporation

ENTRANT
Rapid Displays
Chicago, Illinois

SUB-CATEGORY
Computer Hardware

DIVISION
Semi-Permanent

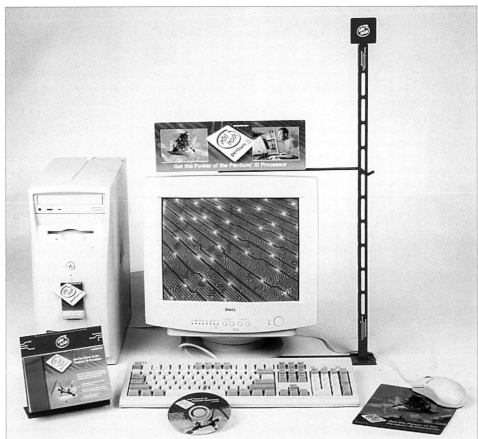

AWARD
Bronze

TITLE
Banjo Tooie Standee

CLIENT
Nintendo of America

ENTRANT
CRP/NW – D/B/A The Corporate Image
Seattle, Washington

SUB-CATEGORY
Home Entertainment – Interactive, Motion,
or Illuminated

DIVISION
Semi-Permanent

AWARD
Bronze

TITLE
Microsoft Shelf Display for
Office Max Stores

CLIENT
Microsoft Corporation

ENTRANT
Design Phase, Inc.
Northbrook, Illinois

SUB-CATEGORY
Computer Software

DIVISION
Semi-Permanent

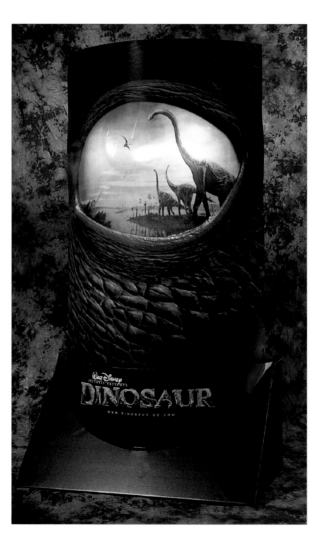

AWARD
Bronze

TITLE
Illuminated Dinosaur Standee

CLIENT
Walt Disney Studios

ENTRANT
Rapid Displays
Chicago, Illinois

SUB-CATEGORY
Movies, Tapes, Records, CDs

DIVISION
Semi-Permanent

AWARD
Bronze

TITLE
Bedazzled

CLIENT
Twentieth Century Fox

ENTRANT
Drissi Advertising
Los Angeles, California

SUB-CATEGORY
Movies, Tapes, Records, CDs

DIVISION
Semi-Permanent

AWARD
Bronze

TITLE
Pentium III Fall Launch

CLIENT
Intel Corporation

ENTRANT
Rapid Displays
Chicago, Illinois

SUB-CATEGORY
Computer Hardware

DIVISION
Semi-Permanent

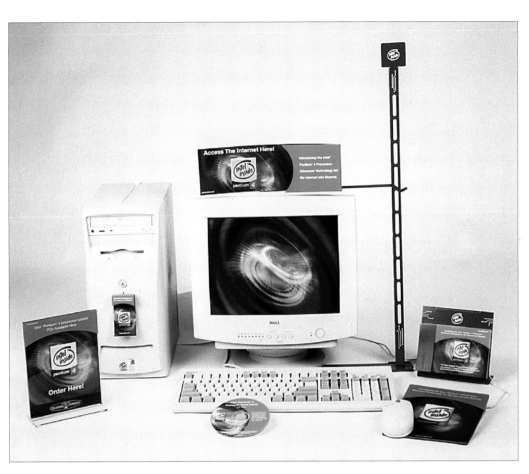

AWARD
Bronze

TITLE
Airport Flipbook Display

CLIENT
March First

ENTRANT
Rapid Displays
Chicago, Illinois

SUB-CATEGORY
Computer Hardware

DIVISION
Semi-Permanent

Entertainment and Computers

AWARD
Gold

TITLE
Toy Story 2 Floor Display

CLIENT
Buena Vista Home Entertainment

ENTRANT
Origin, LLC.
Burbank, California

SUB-CATEGORY
Movies, Tapes, Records, CDs

DIVISION
Temporary

AWARD
Gold

TITLE
The Tigger Movie Floor Display

CLIENT
Buena Vista Home Entertainment

ENTRANT
Origin, LLC.
Burbank, California

SUB-CATEGORY
Movies, Tapes, Records, CDs

DIVISION
Temporary

AWARD
Silver

TITLE
Driven

CLIENT
Warner Brothers

ENTRANT
Drissi Advertising
Los Angeles, California

SUB-CATEGORY
Movies, Tapes, Records, CDs

DIVISION
Temporary

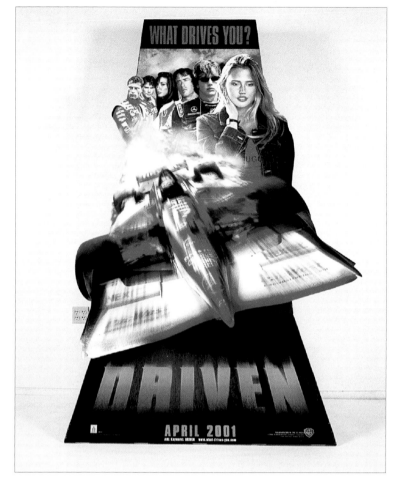

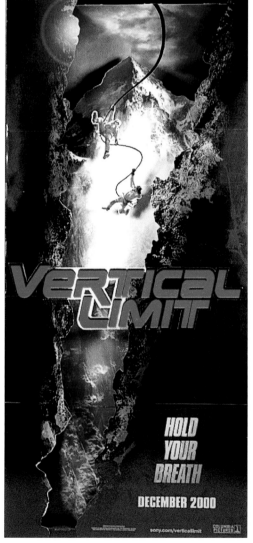

AWARD
Silver

TITLE
Vertical Limit

CLIENT
Columbia Pictures

ENTRANT
Drissi Advertising
Los Angeles, California

SUB-CATEGORY
Movies, Tapes, Records, CDs

DIVISION
Temporary

AWARD
Bronze

TITLE
Tarzan Arch Display

CLIENT
Buena Vista Home Entertainment

ENTRANT
Smurfit-Stone Display Group and
Cameo Container
Chicago, Illinois

SUB-CATEGORY
Movies, Tapes, Records, CDs

DIVISION
Temporary

AWARD
Bronze

TITLE
Fantasia Standee

CLIENT
Buena Vista Home Entertainment

ENTRANT
Cornerstone Display Group Inc.
San Fernando, California

SUB-CATEGORY
Movies, Tapes, Records, CDs

DIVISION
Temporary

AWARD
Bronze

TITLE
Little Mermaid Video Standee

CLIENT
Buena Vista Home Entertainment

ENTRANT
Cornerstone Display Group Inc.
San Fernando, California

SUB-CATEGORY
Movies, Tapes, Records, CDs

DIVISION
Temporary

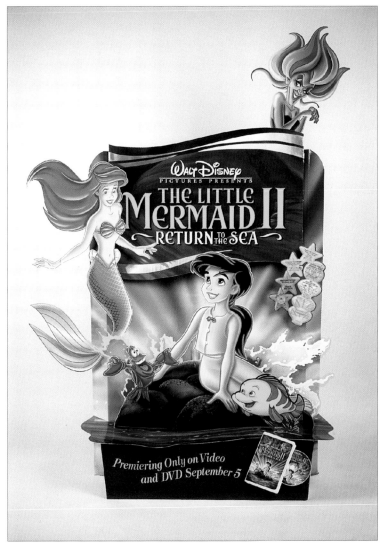

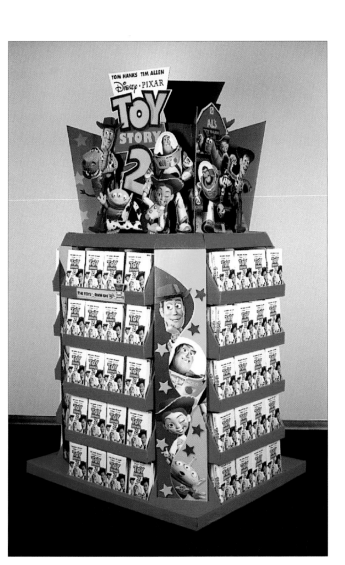

AWARD
Bronze

TITLE
Toy Story II "Magna" Merchandiser

CLIENT
Buena Vista Home Entertainment

ENTRANT
Cornerstone Display Group Inc.
and Cameo Container
San Fernando, California

SUB-CATEGORY
Movies, Tapes, Records, CDs

DIVISION
Temporary

Entertainment and Computers

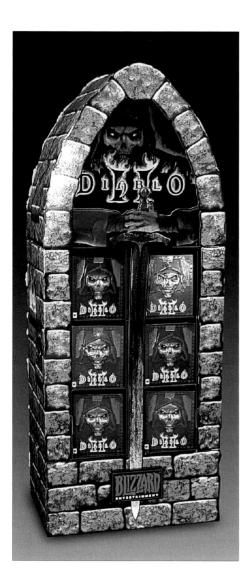

AWARD
Bronze

TITLE
Diablo® II Shrine Floor Display

CLIENT
Havas Interactive/Blizzard
Entertainment

ENTRANT
Justman Packaging & Display
Los Angeles, California

SUB-CATEGORY
Computer Software

DIVISION
Temporary

AWARD
Bronze

TITLE
Chicken Run Floor Display

CLIENT
DreamWorks,
SKG Home Entertainment

ENTRANT
Origin, LLC.
Burbank, California

SUB-CATEGORY
Movies, Tapes, Records, CDs

DIVISION
Temporary

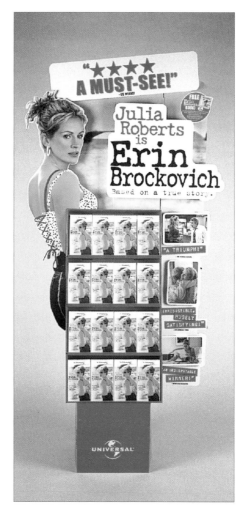

AWARD
Bronze

TITLE
Erin Brockovich Floor Display

CLIENT
Universal Home Entertainment

ENTRANT
Origin, LLC.
Burbank, California

SUB-CATEGORY
Movies, Tapes, Records, CDs

DIVISION
Temporary

AWARD
Gold

TITLE
Fragrance Bar Cds (1 To 5 Units)

CLIENT
Parfums Christian Dior

ENTRANT
Diam Group
Les Mureaux, France

SUB-CATEGORY
Men's and Women's Colognes,
Fragrances, Eau de Toilette, etc.

DIVISION
Permanent

AWARD
Silver

TITLE
The Ralph Counter Display

CLIENT
L'Oréal USA

ENTRANT
Consumer Promotions International
Mount Vernon, New York

SUB-CATEGORY
Women's Perfumes

DIVISION
Permanent

Fragrances

AWARD
Bronze

TITLE
Nautica Latitude/Longitude
Display Program

CLIENT
Unilever Cosmetics International

ENTRANT
The Royal Promotion Group Inc.
New York, New York

SUB-CATEGORY
Men's and Women's Colognes,
Fragrances, Eau de Toilette, etc.

DIVISION
Permanent

AWARD
Bronze

TITLE
Estée Lauder Compact Display

CLIENT
Estée Lauder Corporation

ENTRANT
Trans World Marketing
East Rutherford, New Jersey

SUB-CATEGORY
Men's and Women's Colognes,
Fragrances, Eau de Toilette, etc.

DIVISION
Permanent

AWARD
Gold

TITLE
Giorgio Beverly Hills "G" Displays

CLIENT
Procter & Gamble Prestige Beauté

ENTRANT
Diam International Ltd.
Loughborough, Leicestershire, United
Kingdom

SUB-CATEGORY
Women's Perfumes

DIVISION
Semi-Permanent

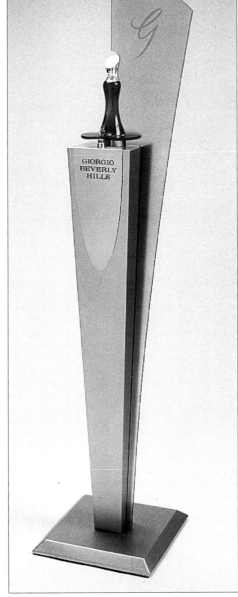

AWARD
Silver

TITLE
Puig Ultra Violet Display Box

CLIENT
Puig USA

ENTRANT
The Royal Promotion Group Inc.
New York, New York

SUB-CATEGORY
Women's Perfumes

DIVISION
Temporary

AWARD
Silver

TITLE
Boss Woman Displays

CLIENT
Procter & Gamble Prestige Beauté

ENTRANT
Diam International Ltd.
Loughborough, Leicestershire,
United Kingdom

SUB-CATEGORY
Women's Perfumes
Temporary

Grocery and General Merchandise Products

AWARD
Gold

TITLE
General Mills Snack Display

CLIENT
General Mills

ENTRANT
Gage In-Store Marketing
Minneapolis, Minnesota

SUB-CATEGORY
Containerized and Processed Foods

DIVISION
Permanent

AWARD
Silver

TITLE
Lunchables Tray Merchandiser

CLIENT
Oscar Mayer Foods

ENTRANT
DCI Marketing
Milwaukee, Wisconsin

SUB-CATEGORY
Frozen, Fresh, and Refrigerated
Foods

DIVISION
Permanent

AWARD
Bronze

TITLE
Hormel Foods Modular
Meat Products Tower

CLIENT
Hormel Foods Corporation

ENTRANT
Advertising Display Company
Lyndhurst, New Jersey

SUB-CATEGORY
Containerized and Processed
Foods

DIVISION
Permanent

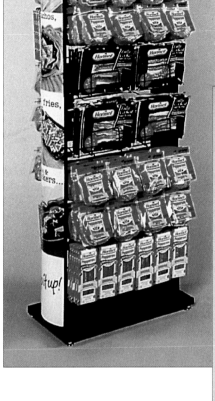

AWARD
Silver

TITLE
Nestle-Ortega Merchandising
Center

CLIENT
Nestle USA

ENTRANT
Chesapeake Display & Packaging Co.
Winston-Salem, North Carolina

SUB-CATEGORY
Containerized and Processed Foods

DIVISION
Semi-Permanent

Grocery and General Merchandise Products

AWARD
Bronze

TITLE
KIWI Blue Bubbles Floor Display

CLIENT
Sara Lee Taiwan

ENTRANT
AimAsia Integrated Marketing Network Ltd.
Taipei, Taiwan, R.O.C.

SUB-CATEGORY
Paper Goods and Soap

DIVISION
Semi-Permanent

AWARD
Gold

TITLE
La-Z-Boy Armchair Display

CLIENT
Paramount Farms

ENTRANT
Justman Packaging & Display
Los Angeles, California

SUB-CATEGORY
Frozen, Fresh, and Refrigerated
Foods

DIVISION
Temporary

AWARD
Bronze

TITLE
Heinz Holiday Tree Display

CLIENT
Heinz Pet Products

ENTRANT
Inland Paperboard & Packaging
Indianapolis, Indiana

SUB-CATEGORY
Pet Food and Accessories

DIVISION
Temporary

AWARD
Bronze

TITLE
Best Foods–Squeezables Display

CLIENT
Best Foods

ENTRANT
Smurfit-Image Pac-MBI
Toronto, Ontario, Canada

SUB-CATEGORY
Containerized and Processed Foods

DIVISION
Temporary

Hair and Skin Care

AWARD
Gold

TITLE
@tmosphere Floor Display

CLIENT
Morlee Group

ENTRANT
Point 1 Displays Inc.
Montreal, Quebec, Canada

SUB-CATEGORY
Skin Care Products

DIVISION
Permanent

AWARD
Silver

TITLE
Calgon 2 oz. Body Lotion Bath Tub

CLIENT
Coty

ENTRANT
Advertising Display Company
Lyndhurst, New Jersey

SUB-CATEGORY
Suntan Products, Lotions, Moisturizers,
and Creams

DIVISION
Permanent

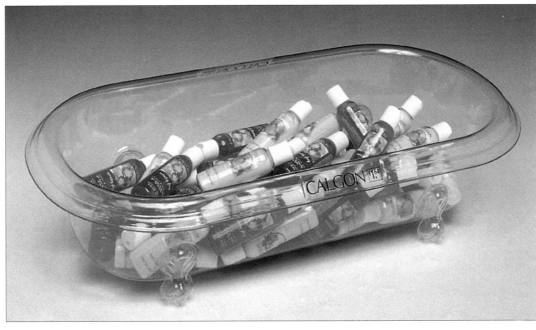

AWARD
Silver

TITLE
Elizabeth Arden Treatment Floor Display

CLIENT
Elizabeth Arden Company

ENTRANT
Consumer Promotions International
Mount Vernon, New York

SUB-CATEGORY
Suntan Products, Lotions, Moisturizers,
and Creams

DIVISION
Permanent

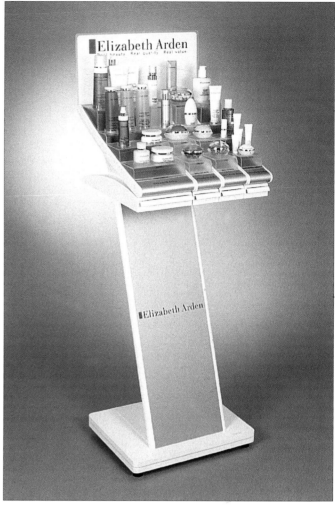

AWARD
Silver

TITLE
Sarah Michaels/Nature's Accents Inline Sys.

CLIENT
The Dial Corporation

ENTRANT
The Niven Marketing Group
Bensenville, Illinois

SUB-CATEGORY
Skin Care Products

DIVISION
Permanent

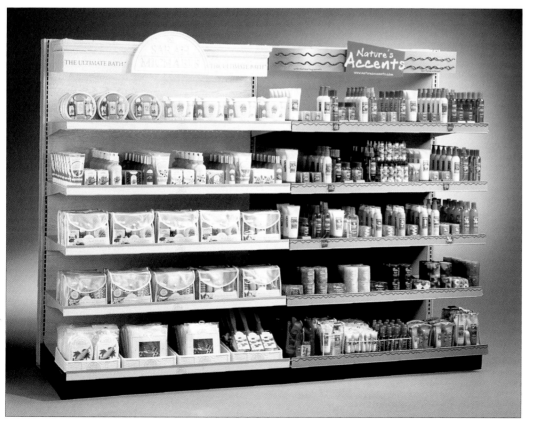

Hair and Skin Care

AWARD
Bronze

TITLE
Physique Traveling Kiosk

CLIENT
Procter & Gamble

ENTRANT
Array Marketing Group /IDMD Design
& Manufacturing
Toronto, Ontario, Canada

SUB-CATEGORY
Hair Styling and Coloring Products

DIVISION
Permanent

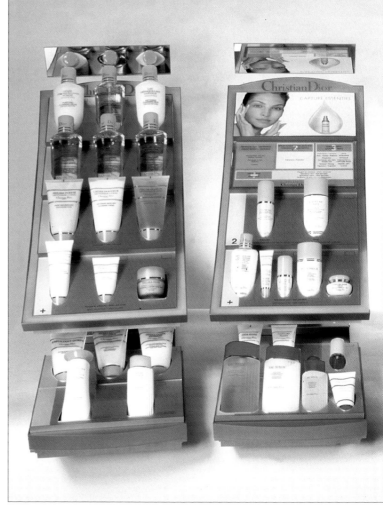

AWARD
Bronze

TITLE
Skincare Bar Cds (1 To 5 Units)

CLIENT
Parfums Christian Dior

ENTRANT
Diam Group
Les Mureaux, France

SUB-CATEGORY
Skin Care Products

DIVISION
Permanent

AWARD
Bronze

TITLE
Skincare GTS Color Dynamic System

CLIENT
Parfums Christian Dior

ENTRANT
Diam Group
Les Mureaux, France

SUB-CATEGORY
Suntan Products, Lotions,
Moisturizers, and Creams

DIVISION
Permanent

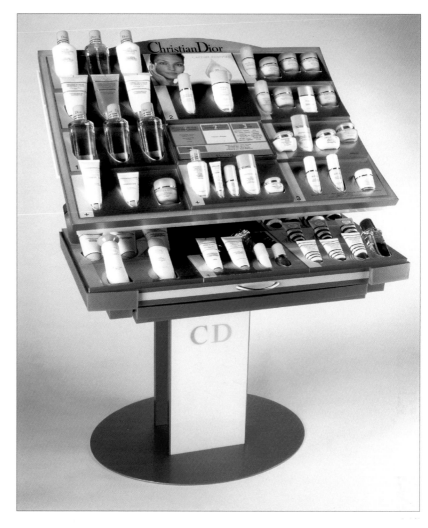

AWARD
Bronze

TITLE
Pantene Panacea Permanent Endcap

CLIENT
The Procter & Gamble Company

ENTRANT
Henschel-Steinau, Inc.
Englewood, New Jersey

SUB-CATEGORY
Hair Cleansing Treatments

DIVISION
Permanent

Hair and Skin Care

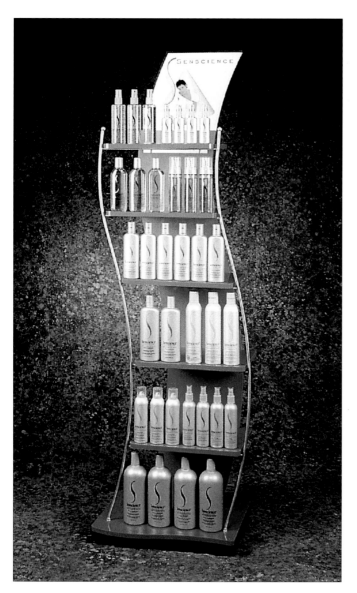

AWARD
Bronze

TITLE
Senscience Floor Display

CLIENT
Zotos International

ENTRANT
Point 1 Displays Inc.
Montreal, Quebec, Canada

SUB-CATEGORY
Hair Cleansing Treatments

DIVISION
Permanent

AWARD
Bronze

TITLE
RUSK Source 2000 Salon Rack

CLIENT
Rusk Inc.

ENTRANT
The Display Link Inc.
Babylon, New York

SUB-CATEGORY
Hair Cleansing Treatments

DIVISION
Permanent

AWARD
Gold

TITLE
Pantene Panacea 142 pc. Tower

CLIENT
The Procter & Gamble Company

ENTRANT
Henschel-Steinau, Inc.
Englewood, New Jersey

SUB-CATEGORY
Hair Cleansing Treatments

DIVISION
Semi-Permanent

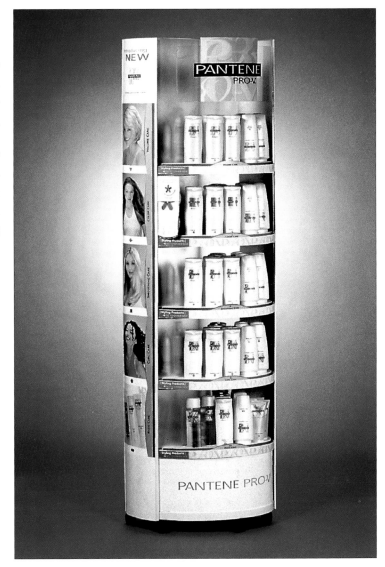

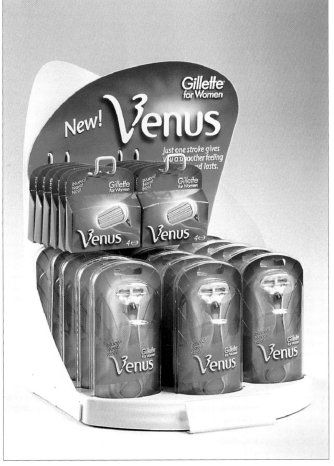

AWARD
Silver

TITLE
Venus Launch Display Program

CLIENT
The Gillette Company

ENTRANT
Diam International Ltd. and ADC
Loughborough, Leicestershire, United
Kingdom

SUB-CATEGORY
Brushes, Hairdryers, Razors, and Combs

DIVISION
Semi-Permanent

AWARD
Silver

TITLE
Candy Kisses Jungle Display

CLIENT
Beautycology, Inc.

ENTRANT
Triangle Display Group
Philadelphia, Pennsylvania

SUB-CATEGORY
Skin Care Products

DIVISION
Semi-Permanent

AWARD
Bronze

TITLE
L'Oréal Plenitude Hydra Fresh
Counter Display

CLIENT
L'Oréal, Inc

ENTRANT
Display Producers Inc.
Bronx, New York

SUB-CATEGORY
Suntan Products, Lotions,
Moisturizers, and Creams

DIVISION
Semi-Permanent

AWARD
Bronze

TITLE
Braun Syncro System Shaver
Pallet Display

CLIENT
The Gillette Company

ENTRANT
Kendall King Graphics
Kansas City, Kansas

SUB-CATEGORY
Brushes, Hairdryers, Razors,
and Combs

DIVISION
Semi-Permanent

AWARD
Bronze

TITLE
Chap Stick Wal-Mart
Gravity Feed Power Wing

CLIENT
Whitehall-Robins

ENTRANT
Henschel-Steinau, Inc.
Englewood, New Jersey

SUB-CATEGORY
Suntan Products, Lotions,
Moisturizers, and Creams

DIVISION
Semi-Permanent

AWARD
Bronze

TITLE
L'Oréal Revitalift Slim Line
Eraser Mini-Wing

CLIENT
L'Oréal Cosmetics &
Fragrances Division

ENTRANT
Ultimate Display Industries Inc.
Jamaica, New York

SUB-CATEGORY
Suntan Products, Lotions,
Moisturizers, and Creams

DIVISION
Semi-Permanent

Hair and Skin Care

AWARD
Gold

TITLE
Edge Display

CLIENT
Groupe Everest

ENTRANT
Techno P.O.S. Inc.
Montreal, Quebec, Canada

SUB-CATEGORY
Skin Care Products

DIVISION
Temporary

AWARD
Silver

TITLE
Nature's Accents Bath Treats
Counter Display

CLIENT
The Dial Corporation

ENTRANT
Henschel-Steinau, Inc.
Englewood, New Jersey

SUB-CATEGORY
Skin Care Products

DIVISION
Temporary

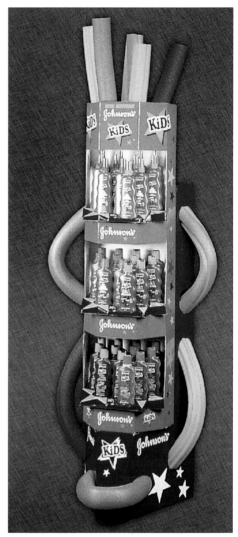

AWARD
Bronze

TITLE
Vaseline Intensive Care 1oz.
Counter Display

CLIENT
Unilever HPC – USA

ENTRANT
Advertising Display Company
Lyndhurst, New Jersey

SUB-CATEGORY
Suntan Products, Lotions,
Moisturizers, and Creams

DIVISION
Temporary

AWARD
Silver

TITLE
Herbal Essences Facial Care

CLIENT
Bristol Myers Squibb

ENTRANT
Techno P.O.S. Inc.
Montreal, Quebec, Canada

SUB-CATEGORY
Suntan Products, Lotions,
Moisturizers, and Creams

DIVISION
Temporary

AWARD
Silver

TITLE
Johnson & Johnson
Kids Summer Display

CLIENT
Johnson & Johnson, Inc.

ENTRANT
Point 1 Displays Inc.
Montreal, Quebec, Canada

SUB-CATEGORY
Hair Cleansing Treatments

DIVISION
Temporary

AWARD
Bronze

TITLE
Chapstick Gravity PDQ #817050

CLIENT
Whitehall-Robins, Div. of American Home Prod.

ENTRANT
Oxford Innovations
New Oxford, Pennsylvania

SUB-CATEGORY
Suntan Products, Lotions, Moisturizers, and
Creams

DIVISION
Temporary

AWARD
Bronze

TITLE
Johnson & Johnson Kids Fall Display

CLIENT
Johnson & Johnson, Inc.

ENTRANT
Point 1 Displays Inc.
Montreal, Quebec, Canada

SUB-CATEGORY
Hair Cleansing Treatments

DIVISION
Temporary

AWARD
Bronze

TITLE
Herbal Essence Floor Display

CLIENT
Bristol Myers Squibb

ENTRANT
Point 1 Displays Inc.
Montreal, Quebec, Canada

SUB-CATEGORY
Hair Styling and Coloring Products

DIVISION
Temporary

AWARD
Bronze

TITLE
Santa Candy Cane Lip Balm Display

CLIENT
Beautycology, Inc.

ENTRANT
Triangle Display Group
Philadelphia, Pennsylvania

SUB-CATEGORY
Skin Care Products

DIVISION
Temporary

Health Care

AWARD
Gold

TITLE
Infant Formula Free Standing Merchandisier

CLIENT
PBM Products

ENTRANT
Applied Merchandising Concepts, Inc.
New Rochelle, New York

SUB-CATEGORY
Personal Hygiene, Diapers, and Baby Care Items

DIVISION
Permanent

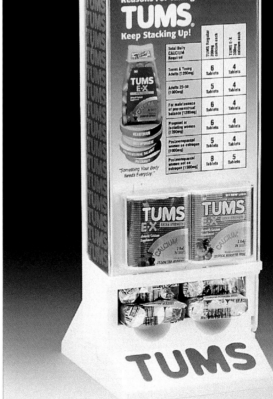

AWARD
Silver

TITLE
Tums 3-Roll Gravity Feed Rack

CLIENT
SmithKline Beecham Consumer Healthcare

ENTRANT
Henschel-Steinau, Inc.
Englewood, New Jersey

SUB-CATEGORY
First Aid and Pharmaceutical

DIVISION
Permanent

AWARD
Bronze

TITLE
Johnson & Johnson Vistakon
Display Program

CLIENT
Johnson & Johnson Vistakon Products, Inc.

ENTRANT
Consumer Promotions International
Mount Vernon, New York

SUB-CATEGORY
First Aid and Pharmaceutical

DIVISION
Permanent

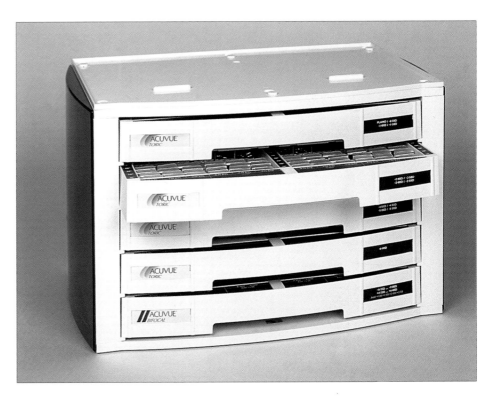

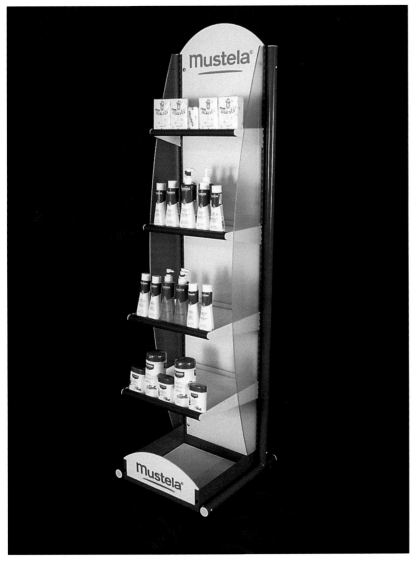

AWARD
Bronze

TITLE
Mustela Wall Stand

CLIENT
Mustela

ENTRANT
Lingo Manufacturing Company, Inc.
Florence, Kentucky

SUB-CATEGORY
Personal Hygiene, Diapers,
and Baby Care Items

DIVISION
Permanent

Health Care

AWARD
Silver

TITLE
Zantac75/Rolaids Firefighter Display

CLIENT
Pfizer/Warner-Lambert Consumer
Healthcare

ENTRANT
Harding Display Corp.
Toronto, Ontario, Canada

SUB-CATEGORY
First Aid and Pharmaceutical

DIVISION
Semi-Permanent

AWARD
Bronze

TITLE
Arm and Hammer Family of Floorstands

CLIENT
Church & Dweight Co., Inc.

ENTRANT
Phoenix Display/International Paper
Thorofare, New Jersey

SUB-CATEGORY
Dentifirces, Mouthwash,
and Oral care Implements

DIVISION
Semi-Permanent

AWARD
Gold

TITLE
Alluna Sidekick Gravity Feed Display

CLIENT
Smithkline Beecham

ENTRANT
Packaging Specialist
Clinton, Pennsylvania

SUB-CATEGORY
First Aid and Pharmaceutical

DIVISION
Temporary

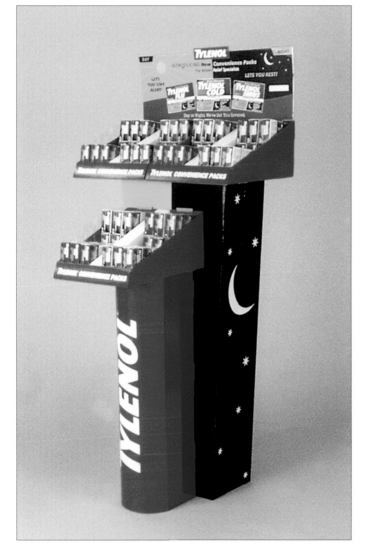

AWARD
Gold

TITLE
Tylenol Winter Relief 2000

CLIENT
McNeil Consumer Products Company

ENTRANT
Techno P.O.S. Inc.
Montreal, Quebec, Canada

SUB-CATEGORY
First Aid and Pharmaceutical

DIVISION
Temporary

Health Care

AWARD
Silver

TITLE
Colgate "KRAD" Racing Display

CLIENT
Busch Creative Services

ENTRANT
Rapid Displays
Chicago, Illinois

SUB-CATEGORY
Dentifirces, Mouthwash, and
Oral care Implements

DIVISION
Temporary

AWARD
Silver

TITLE
Johnson's Kids "Bursting with Fruit" Display

CLIENT
Johnson & Johnson Consumer Companies, Inc.

ENTRANT
Smurfit-Stone Display Group
Carol Stream, Illinois

SUB-CATEGORY
Personal Hygiene, Diapers, and Baby Care Items

DIVISION
Temporary

AWARD
Silver

TITLE
Monistat Floor/Combo Display

CLIENT
McNeil Consumer Products Company

ENTRANT
Techno P.O.S. Inc.
Montreal, Quebec, Canada

SUB-CATEGORY
Personal Hygiene, Diapers,
and Baby Care Items

DIVISION
Temporary

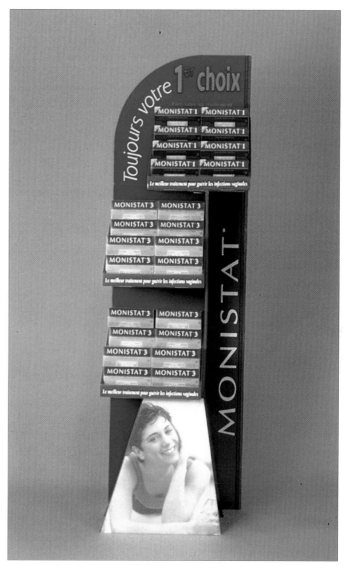

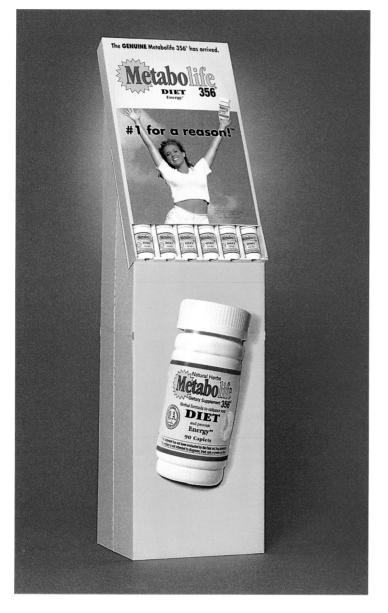

AWARD
Bronze

TITLE
Metabolife Floor Stand

CLIENT
Metabolife International Inc.

ENTRANT
Meridian Display & Merchandising
St. Paul, Minnesota

SUB-CATEGORY
First Aid and Pharmaceutical

DIVISION
Temporary

Health Care

AWARD
Bronze

TITLE
The Dilbert 12 Hour Relief Zone

CLIENT
Schering-Plough HealthCare
Products, Inc.

ENTRANT
Phoenix Display/International Paper
Thorofare, New Jersey

SUB-CATEGORY
First Aid and Pharmaceutical

DIVISION
Temporary

AWARD
Bronze

TITLE
Kodak/Crest Keepsake Promo Floor Display

CLIENT
Kodak Canada

ENTRANT
Protagon Display Inc. and Procter & Gamble
Scarborough, Ontario, Canada

SUB-CATEGORY
Dentifirces, Mouthwash, and Oral care Implements

DIVISION
Temporary

AWARD
Bronze

TITLE
Children's Advil 4 oz. PW/FS

CLIENT
Whitehall-Robins Healthcare

ENTRANT
Smurfit-Stone Display Group
Sandston, Virginia

SUB-CATEGORY
First Aid and Pharmaceutical

DIVISION
Temporary

AWARD
Bronze

TITLE
Johnson's Antibacterial Towelettes Display

CLIENT
Johnson & Johnson Consumer
Companies, Inc.

ENTRANT
Smurfit-Stone Display Group
Carol Stream, Illinois

SUB-CATEGORY
Personal Hygiene, Diapers, and
Baby Care Items

DIVISION
Temporary

Home and Garden

AWARD
Gold

TITLE
Thomasville Cabinetry Lifestyle Galleries

CLIENT
Thomasville Furniture Industries

ENTRANT
Cormark
Elk Grove Village, Illinois

SUB-CATEGORY
Home Furnishings and Housewares

DIVISION
Permanent

AWARD
Gold

TITLE
Fresh Flower Kiosk

CLIENT
Hallmark Cards

ENTRANT
Performance Display, Inc.
Urbandale, Indiana

SUB-CATEGORY
Home Furnishings and Housewares

DIVISION
Permanent

AWARD
Silver

TITLE
Create-A-Castle

CLIENT
York Wallcoverings

ENTRANT
Oxford Innovations
New Oxford, Pennsylvania

SUB-CATEGORY
Home Furnishings and Housewares

DIVISION
Permanent

AWARD
Silver

TITLE
Linea Counter Display

CLIENT
Cooper Lighting

ENTRANT
Rapid Displays
Chicago, Illinois

SUB-CATEGORY
Building Supplies

DIVISION
Permanent

AWARD
Silver

TITLE
Daltile Natural Stone Collection
Display

CLIENT
Dal-Tile Corporation

ENTRANT
Resources Inc. In Display
Cranford, New Jersey

SUB-CATEGORY
Building Supplies

DIVISION
Permanent

AWARD
Silver

TITLE
Sherwin Williams Disney Paint Center

CLIENT
Sherwin Williams

ENTRANT
The Niven Marketing Group
Bensenville, Illinois

SUB-CATEGORY
Building Supplies

DIVISION
Permanent

AWARD
Bronze

TITLE
Imperial Ralph Lauren Display

CLIENT
Imperial Home Decor Group

ENTRANT
AG Industries Inc.
Cleveland, Ohio

SUB-CATEGORY
Home Furnishings and Housewares

DIVISION
Permanent

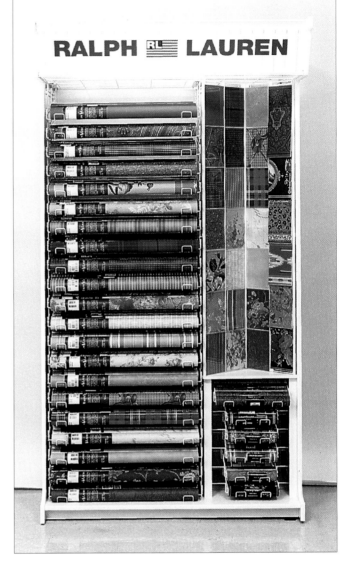

AWARD
Bronze

TITLE
Yamaha Generator Display

CLIENT
Marshall Advertising

ENTRANT
DCI Marketing
Milwaukee, Wisconsin

SUB-CATEGORY
Home and Industrial Tools

DIVISION
Permanent

Home and Garden

AWARD
Bronze

TITLE
Perfect Night Edgelit Sign

CLIENT
Serta, Inc.

ENTRANT
Everbrite, Inc.
Greenfield, Wisconsin

SUB-CATEGORY
Home Furnishings and Housewares

DIVISION
Permanent

AWARD
Bronze

TITLE
Moen Upscale Module Program

CLIENT
Moen Incorporated

ENTRANT
Innovative Marketing Solutions, Inc.
Bensenville, Illinois

SUB-CATEGORY
Building Supplies

DIVISION
Permanent

AWARD
Bronze

TITLE
Home Depot Paint Solutions Center

CLIENT
The Home Depot

ENTRANT
The Niven Marketing Group
Bensenville, Illinois

SUB-CATEGORY
Building Supplies

DIVISION
Permanent

AWARD
Silver

TITLE
Combat Eat, Share, Die Rack & Riser

CLIENT
The Clorox Company

ENTRANT
Henschel-Steinau, Inc.
Englewood, New Jersey

SUB-CATEGORY
Lawn and Garden Supplies

DIVISION
Semi-Permanent

AWARD
Silver

TITLE
Nutrite Plant Fertilizer Floor
Display

CLIENT
Hydro Agri Canada

ENTRANT
Point 1 Displays Inc.
Montreal, Quebec, Canada

SUB-CATEGORY
Lawn and Garden Supplies

DIVISION
Semi-Permanent

AWARD
Bronze

TITLE
Krylon 30 Minute Makeover 2000

CLIENT
Sherwin Williams

ENTRANT
Menasha Display
(A Division of Menasha Corp.)
Mequon, Wisconsin

SUB-CATEGORY
Home and Industrial Tools

DIVISION
Semi-Permanent

AWARD
Bronze

TITLE
Eureka "Stick Vac Bonus" Display

CLIENT
The Eureka Company

ENTRANT
Rapid Displays
Chicago, Illinois

SUB-CATEGORY
Home and Industrial Tools

DIVISION
Semi-Permanent

AWARD
Bronze

TITLE
Burpee Modular Spring Tray Display

CLIENT
W. Atlee Burpee & Co.

ENTRANT
Triangle Display Group
Philadelphia, Pennsylvania

SUB-CATEGORY
Lawn and Garden Supplies

DIVISION
Semi-Permanent

AWARD
Bronze

TITLE
Bayer-Pursell – Quarter Pallet Display

CLIENT
Bayer-Pursell, LLC

ENTRANT
Inland Paperboard & Packaging
Indianapolis, Indiana

SUB-CATEGORY
Lawn and Garden Supplies

DIVISION
Temporary

Interactive

AWARD
Gold

TITLE
Kia Interactive Oval Kiosk K2K

CLIENT
Kia Motors America

ENTRANT
DCI Marketing
Milwaukee, Wisconsin

SUB-CATEGORY
Interactive Category

DIVISION
Permanent

AWARD
Silver

TITLE
Interactive Brand Center

CLIENT
General Motors Corporation

ENTRANT
DCI Marketing
Milwaukee, Wisconsin

SUB-CATEGORY
Interactive Category

DIVISION
Permanent

AWARD
Bronze

TITLE
Palm Family Shelf Display

CLIENT
Palm, Inc.

ENTRANT
Rapid Displays
Chicago, Illinois

SUB-CATEGORY
Interactive Category

DIVISION
Permanent

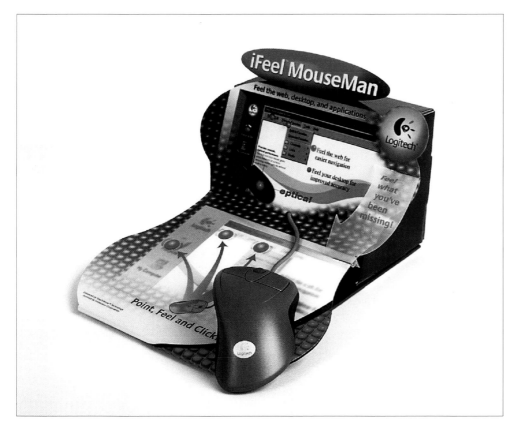

AWARD
Silver

TITLE
iFeel MouseMan Display

CLIENT
Logitech

ENTRANT
Rapid Displays
Chicago, Illinois

SUB-CATEGORY
Interactive Category

DIVISION
Semi-Permanent

AWARD
Gold

TITLE
Dinner On Hand
Permanent Merchandiser

CLIENT
Kraft Foods, Inc.

ENTRANT
Henschel-Steinau, Inc
Englewood, New Jersey

SUB-CATEGORY
Mass Merchandise Retailer
(Traditional/Super Center)

DIVISION
Permanent

AWARD
Silver

TITLE
Disney/Wal-Mart Watch
Merchandising Program

CLIENT
SII Marketing International

ENTRANT
Chicago Show Inc.
Northfield, Illinois

SUB-CATEGORY
Mass Merchandise Retailer
(Traditional/Super Center)

DIVISION
Permanent

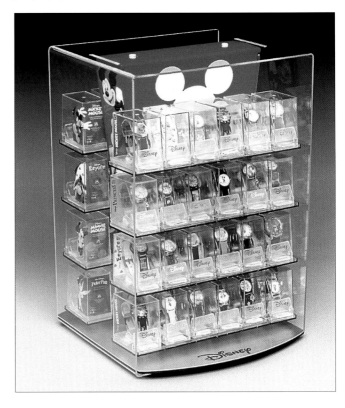

AWARD
Silver

TITLE
BlueLight.com Countertop Kiosk

CLIENT
BlueLight.com

ENTRANT
DCI Marketing
Milwaukee, Wisconsin

SUB-CATEGORY
Mass Merchandise Retailer
(Traditional/Super Center)

DIVISION
Permanent

AWARD
Bronze

TITLE
Lowe's Alexander Julian
Wallpaper Fixture

CLIENT
Lowe's

ENTRANT
CDA Industries Inc.
Pickering, Ontario, Canada

SUB-CATEGORY
Mass Merchandise Retailer
(Traditional/Super Center)

DIVISION
Permanent

AWARD
Bronze

TITLE
P&G/Lyrick Studios Barney Luvs
Merchandiser

CLIENT
Lyrick Studios

ENTRANT
Phoenix Display/International Paper
Thorofare, New Jersey

SUB-CATEGORY
Mass Merchandise Retailer
(Traditional/Super Center)

DIVISION
Permanent

Mass Merchandise Retailer

AWARD
Silver

TITLE
Sears Presents Franklin the Turtle

CLIENT
Nova Marketing Communications

ENTRANT
C.D. Baird & Co., Inc. and
Sears, Roebuck & Co
West Allis, Wisconsin

SUB-CATEGORY
Mass Merchandise Retailer
(Traditional/Super Center)

DIVISION
Semi-Permanent

AWARD
Bronze

TITLE
The Grinch's Holiday
Whobilation

CLIENT
Universal Studios Consumer
Products Group

ENTRANT
Diam International
Loughborough, Leicestershire,
United Kingdom

SUB-CATEGORY
Mass Merchandise Retailer
(Traditional/Super Center

DIVISION
Temporary

AWARD
Gold

TITLE
QuickCam Internet Camera Pallet Display

CLIENT
Logitech, Inc.

ENTRANT
Protagon Display, Inc.
Scarborough Ontario, Canada

SUB-CATEGORY
Other Retailer

DIVISION
Permanent

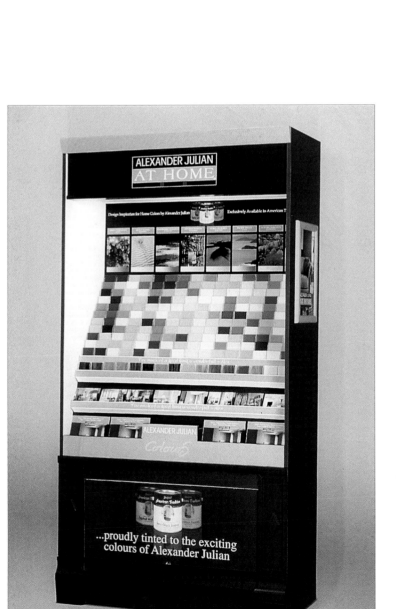

AWARD
Silver

TITLE
Lowe's/Alexander Julian Paint
Decorating System

CLIENT
Valspar Corp.

ENTRANT
The Niven Marketing Group
Bensenville, Illinois

SUB-CATEGORY
Other Retailer

DIVISION
Permanent

Other Retailer

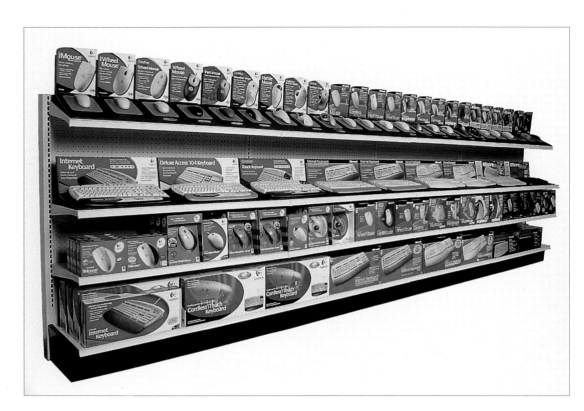

AWARD
Bronze

TITLE
Staples Mouse/Keyboard Cateory Management

CLIENT
Logitech, Inc.

ENTRANT
Protagon Display, Inc.
Scarborough, Ontario, Canada

SUB-CATEGORY
Other Retailer

DIVISION
Permanent

AWARD
Bronze

TITLE
Home Depot Lock Aisle

CLIENT
Home Depot

ENTRANT
Trans World Marketing
East Rutherford, New Jersey

SUB-CATEGORY
Other Retailer

DIVISION
Permanent

AWARD
Silver

TITLE
Nature's Recipe Dog Kiosk

CLIENT
Heinz

ENTRANT
NOW Corporation
Alamo, California

SUB-CATEGORY
Other Retailer

DIVISION
Semi-Permanent

AWARD
Gold

TITLE
Logitech Full-Line Display for Office Depot

CLIENT
Logitech, Inc.

ENTRANT
Protagon Display, Inc.
Scarborough, Ontario, Canada

SUB-CATEGORY
Other Retailer

DIVISION
Temporary

AWARD
Silver

TITLE
Penguins Prelude and
Penguins Video Display

CLIENT
Big Idea

ENTRANT
Rapid Displays
Union City, California

SUB-CATEGORY
Other Retailer

DIVISION
Temporary

AWARD
Bronze

TITLE
Spalding Etonic Golf Glove Display

CLIENT
Spalding Sports Worldwide

ENTRANT
Smurfit-Stone Display Group
Sandston, Virginia

SUB-CATEGORY
Other Retailer

DIVISION
Temporary

AWARD
Gold

TITLE
Tissot Vision Watch Display

CLIENT
Tissot SA

ENTRANT
Diam International, Ltd.
Woodside, New York

SUB-CATEGORY
Jewelry

DIVISION
Permanent

AWARD
Gold

TITLE
adidas Leadership Floor Display

CLIENT
adidas America

ENTRANT
JPMS, Inc.
Santa Fe Springs, California

SUB-CATEGORY
Footwear

DIVISION
Permanent

Personal Products and Accessories

Silver

TITLE
Hi-Tec Floor Stand Display

CLIENT
Hi-Tec Sports, USA

ENTRANT
JPMS Inc.
Santa Fe Springs, California

SUB-CATEGORY
Footwear

DIVISION
Permanent

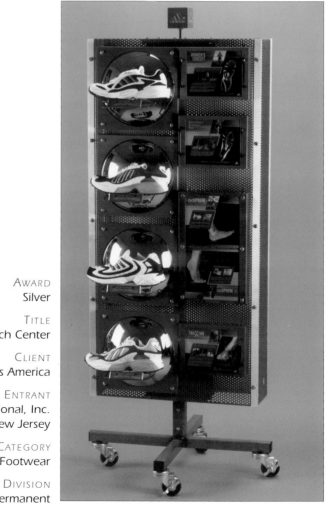

AWARD
Silver

TITLE
adidas Tech Center

CLIENT
Adidas America

ENTRANT
Rand Display International, Inc.
Teaneck, New Jersey

SUB-CATEGORY
Footwear

DIVISION
Permanent

AWARD
Silver

TITLE
Nike Footaction "Urban" Program

CLIENT
Nike, Inc.

ENTRANT
RTC Industries, Inc.
Rolling Meadows, Illinois

SUB-CATEGORY
Footwear

DIVISION
Permanent

AWARD
Silver

TITLE
Maui Jim Titanium

CLIENT
Maui Jim, Inc.

ENTRANT
Visual Marketing, Inc.
Chicago, Illinois

SUB-CATEGORY
Jewelry

DIVISION
Permanent

Personal Products and Accessories

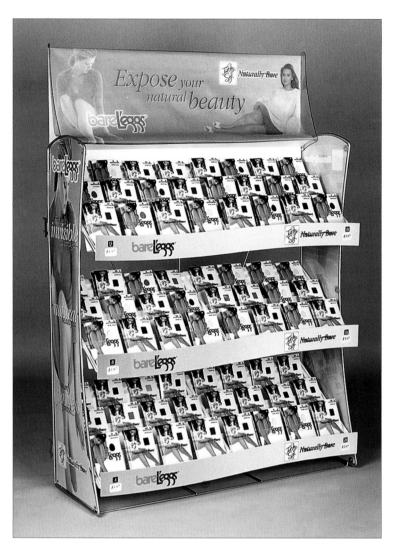

AWARD
Bronze

TITLE
Bare L'eggs/Naturally Bare

CLIENT
Sara Lee Hosiery

ENTRANT
Chesapeake Display & Packaging Co.
Winston-Salem, North Carolina

SUB-CATEGORY
Apparel and Sewing Notions

DIVISION
Permanent

AWARD
Bronze

TITLE
Nike Techlab

CLIENT
Nike, Inc.

ENTRANT
JPMS, Inc.
Santa Fe Springs, California

SUB-CATEGORY
Fine Items and Cameras

DIVISION
Permanent

AWARD
Bronze

TITLE
Skechers USA Collection Tabletop Display

CLIENT
Skechers USA

ENTRANT
United Displaycraft
Des Plaines, Illinois

SUB-CATEGORY
Footwear

DIVISION
Permanent

AWARD
Bronze

TITLE
Skechers USA Journeys Wall &
Lease-Line

CLIENT
Skechers USA

ENTRANT
United Displaycraft
Des Plaines, Illinois

SUB-CATEGORY
Footwear

DIVISION
Permanent

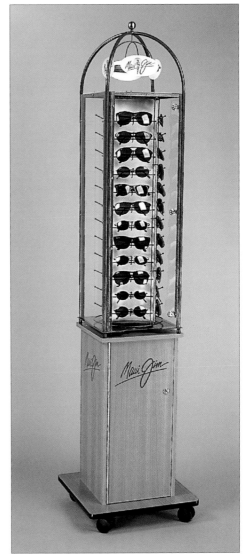

AWARD
Bronze

TITLE
Maui Jim Green Line

CLIENT
Maui Jim, Inc.

ENTRANT
Visual Marketing, Inc.
Chicago, Illinois

SUB-CATEGORY
Jewelry

DIVISION
Permanent

Personal Products and Accessories

AWARD
Gold

TITLE
Old Navy "Kids Club" Merchandiser

CLIENT
Simon Marketing, Inc.

ENTRANT
Packaging Corporation of America
(PCA)
South Gate, California

SUB-CATEGORY
Apparel and Sewing Notions

DIVISION
Semi-Permanent

AWARD
Silver

TITLE
Fall '00 Nike Shox Launch

CLIENT
Nike, Inc.

ENTRANT
Rapid Displays
Union City, Calfornia

SUB-CATEGORY
Footwear

DIVISION
Semi-Permanent

AWARD
Bronze

TITLE
Free 2 Go Wireless by AT&T

CLIENT
AT&T Wireless Services

ENTRANT
AT&T Wireless Services
Paramus, New Jersey

SUB-CATEGORY
Personal Telecommunications

DIVISION
Semi-Permanent

AWARD
Bronze

TITLE
Timber Creek Fathers Day Express Fixture

CLIENT
VF Jeanswear, Inc.

ENTRANT
ImageWorks Display & Marketing Group Inc.
Winston-Salem, North Carolina

SUB-CATEGORY
Apparel and Sewing Notions

DIVISION
Semi-Permanent

Personal Products and Accessories

AWARD
Bronze

TITLE
Qwest Launch Kit

CLIENT
Qwest Wireless

ENTRANT
JPMS, Inc.
Santa Fe Springs, California

SUB-CATEGORY
Personal Telecommunications

DIVISION
Semi-Permanent

AWARD
Bronze

TITLE
SL Holiday Footlocker Window Display

CLIENT
adidas International

ENTRANT
Rapid Displays
Union City, Calfornia

SUB-CATEGORY
Footwear

DIVISION
Semi-Permanent

AWARD
Bronze

TITLE
SL Panels and Shoe Shelves

CLIENT
adidas International

ENTRANT
Rapid Displays
Union City, Calfornia

SUB-CATEGORY
Footwear

DIVISION
Semi-Permanent

AWARD
Bronze

TITLE
Pantymonium Table Topper

CLIENT
Joe Boxer

ENTRANT
Rapid Displays
Union City, California

SUB-CATEGORY
Apparel and Sewing Notions

DIVISION
Semi-Permanent

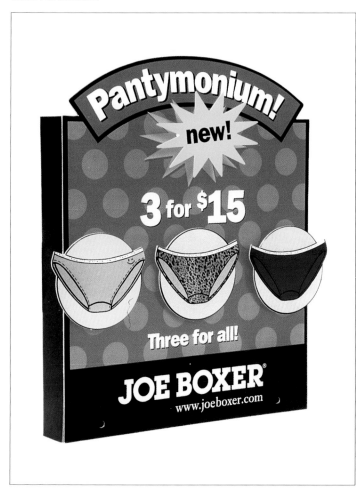

AWARD
Bronze

TITLE
Foot Locker/ Nike Tuned Air – July

CLIENT
Foot Locker

ENTRANT
Medallion Associates Ltd.
New York, New York

SUB-CATEGORY
Footwear

DIVISION
Temporary

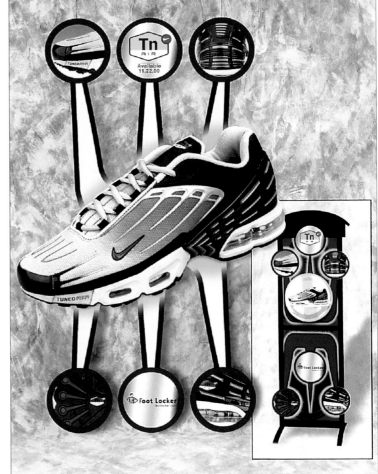

AWARD
Bronze

TITLE
Foot Locker / Nike Tuned Air – November

CLIENT
Foot Locker

ENTRANT
Medallion Associates Ltd.
New York, New York

SUB-CATEGORY
Footwear

DIVISION
Temporary

AWARD
Silver

TITLE
Stoli Afterburner Tour 2000

CLIENT
UDV Stolichnaya

ENTRANT
NOW Corporation
Alamo, California

SUB-CATEGORY
Regional

DIVISION
Permanent

AWARD
Bronze

TITLE
SoBe Adrenaline Rush Counter Merchandiser

CLIENT
South Beach Beverage Co., Inc.

ENTRANT
Joliet Pattern, Inc.
Crest Hill, Illinois

SUB-CATEGORY
National

DIVISION
Permanent

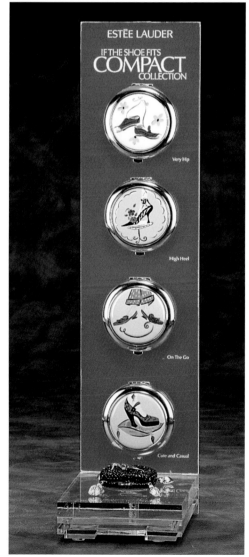

AWARD
Silver

TITLE
Estée Lauder Cinderella Display

CLIENT
Estée Lauder

ENTRANT
Array Marketing Group /IDMD
Design & Manufacturing, Inc.
Toronto, Ontario, Canada

SUB-CATEGORY
Regional

DIVISION
Semi-Permanent

Sales Promotion

AWARD
Bronze

TITLE
Windows Millenium Edition
Launch

CLIENT
Microsoft Corporation

ENTRANT
Ivy Hill Corp. and Levy & Wurz
Glendale, California

SUB-CATEGORY
National

DIVISION
Temporary

AWARD
Bronze

TITLE
Snack Pack Movie Theme Series

CLIENT
ConAgra Grocery Products Company

ENTRANT
Smurfit-Stone Display Group
Sandston, Virginia

SUB-CATEGORY
National

DIVISION
Temporary

Services

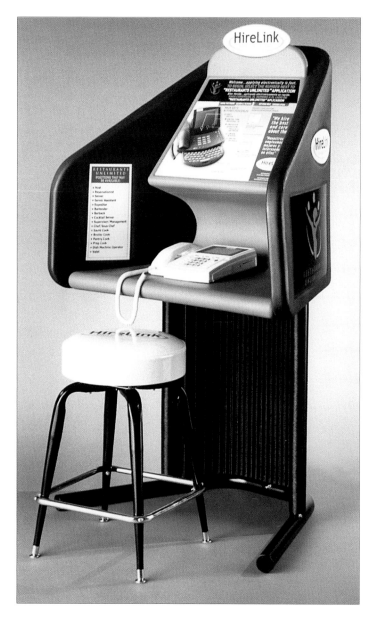

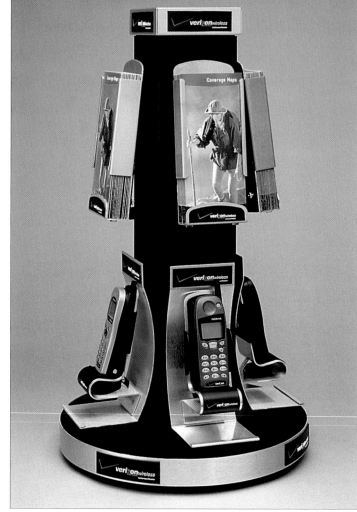

AWARD
Gold

TITLE
Verizon Wireless Pole Display

CLIENT
Verizon Wireless

ENTRANT
Rapid Displays
Union City, Calfornia

SUB-CATEGORY
Professional Services

DIVISION
Permanent

AWARD
Silver

TITLE
IDQ Curly Top® Kid's Meal Display

CLIENT
International Dairy Queen, Inc.

ENTRANT
DCI Marketing
Milwaukee, Wisconsin

SUB-CATEGORY
Quick Service Food Restaurants

DIVISION
Permanent

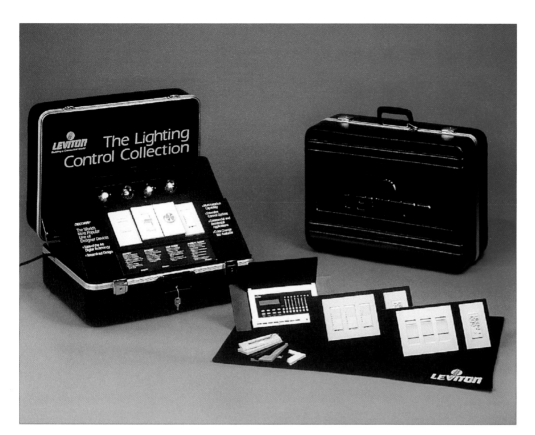

AWARD
Silver

TITLE
Leviton Mobile Dimmer Demo Case

CLIENT
Leviton

ENTRANT
The Display Link, Inc.
Babylon, New York

SUB-CATEGORY
Other Service Establishments

DIVISION
Permanent

AWARD
Bronze

TITLE
Coca-Cola 24″ Synergy Logo

CLIENT
Schwarz Worldwide

ENTRANT
Joliet Pattern, Inc.
Crest Hill, Illinois

SUB-CATEGORY
Quick Service Food Restaurants

DIVISION
Permanent

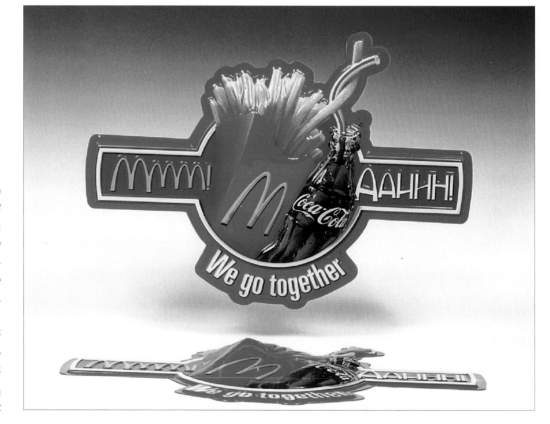

AWARD
Bronze

TITLE
65″ Synergy Coke Bottle

CLIENT
Schwarz Worldwide

ENTRANT
Joliet Pattern, Inc.
Crest Hill, Illinois

SUB-CATEGORY
Quick Service Food Restaurants

DIVISION
Permanent

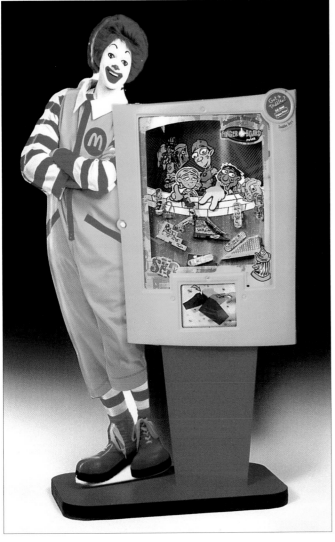

AWARD
Bronze

TITLE
Ronald McDonald Merchandiser

CLIENT
Schwarz Worldwide

ENTRANT
Joliet Pattern, Inc. and Frankel
Crest Hill, Illinois

SUB-CATEGORY
Quick Service Food Restaurants

DIVISION
Permanent

AWARD
Gold

TITLE
McDonald's Yomega Yo-Yo Kiosk

CLIENT
Schwarz Worldwide for McDonald's
Corporation

ENTRANT
Rapid Displays
Union City, Calfornia

SUB-CATEGORY
Quick Service Food Restaurants

DIVISION
Temporary

AWARD
Silver

TITLE
McDonald's Disney Cruise Kiosk

CLIENT
Schwarz Worldwide for
McDonalds Corporation

ENTRANT
Rapid Displays
Union City, Calfornia

SUB-CATEGORY
Quick Service Food Restaurants

DIVISION
Temporary

AWARD
Bronze

TITLE
Rugrats In Paris Floor Display

CLIENT
Alcone Marketing Group/Burger King Corp.

ENTRANT
Justman Packaging & Display
Los Angeles, California

SUB-CATEGORY
Quick Service Food Restaurants

DIVISION
Temporary

AWARD
Bronze

TITLE
Taco Bell Mucho Grande Nachos Display

CLIENT
Impiric

ENTRANT
Rapid Displays
Union City, Calfornia

SUB-CATEGORY
Quick Service Food Restaurants

DIVISION
Temporary

Signage

AWARD
Gold

TITLE
Distortionally Printed Vending
Machine Panels

CLIENT
Coca-Cola South Pacific

ENTRANT
Airform International Limited
Christchurch, Canterbury, New
Zealand

SUB-CATEGORY
Illuminated

DIVISION
Permanent

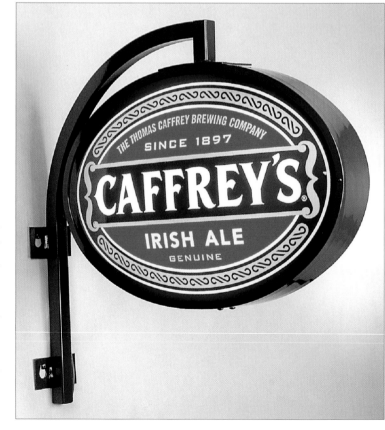

AWARD
Bronze

TITLE
Caffrey's Globe Sign

CLIENT
Guinness Bass Import Company

ENTRANT
Everbrite, Inc.
Greenfield, Wisconsin

SUB-CATEGORY
Illuminated

DIVISION
Permanent

AWARD
Bronze

TITLE
Michelob Light Silhouette Bottle Neon

CLIENT
Anheuser-Busch

ENTRANT
Everbrite, Inc.
Greenfield. Wisconsin

SUB-CATEGORY
Illuminated

DIVISION
Permanent

AWARD
Bronze

TITLE
Western Union Two-Sided Poster Holder

CLIENT
Western Union North America

ENTRANT
Everbrite, Inc.
Greenfield, Wisconsin

SUB-CATEGORY
Non-Illuminated

DIVISION
Permanent

Signage

AWARD
Bronze

TITLE
Coca-Cola Synergy Drive-Thru Presell

CLIENT
Schwarz Worldwide

ENTRANT
Joliet Pattern, Inc.
Crest Hill, Illinois

SUB-CATEGORY
Non-Illuminated

DIVISION
Permanent

AWARD
Bronze

TITLE
K'NEX Sonic Fighter Mobile

CLIENT
K'NEX

ENTRANT
Taurus Display Corporation
Cherry Hill, New Jersey

SUB-CATEGORY
Non-Illuminated

DIVISION
Semi-Permanent

AWARD
Gold

TITLE
Bissell "Proheat" Moire Sign

CLIENT
Bissell

ENTRANT
Rapid Displays
Union City, Calfornia

SUB-CATEGORY
Non-Illuminated

DIVISION
Temporary

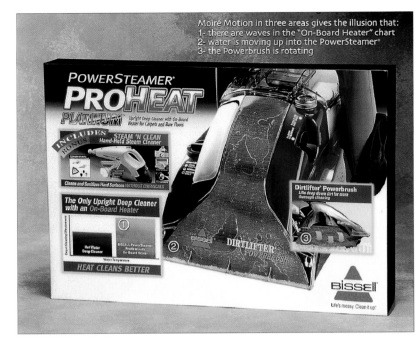

AWARD
Bronze

TITLE
B Dalton Holiday

CLIENT
B Dalton

ENTRANT
Medallion Associates Ltd.
New York, New York

SUB-CATEGORY
Non-Illuminated

DIVISION
Temporary

AWARDAWARD
Bronze

TITLE
Bud Hunting 3D Wall Form

CLIENT
Anheuser-Busch, Inc.

ENTRANT
Anheuser-Busch, Inc.
St. Louis, Missouri

SUB-CATEGORY
Non-Illuminated

DIVISION
Temporary

AWARD
Gold

TITLE
Perrier Poland Springs Crate Display

CLIENT
Perrier Group of America

ENTRANT
Lingo Manufacturing Company, Inc.
Florence, Kentucky

SUB-CATEGORY
Soft Drinks, Mineral Water,
and Powdered Mixes

DIVISION
Permanent

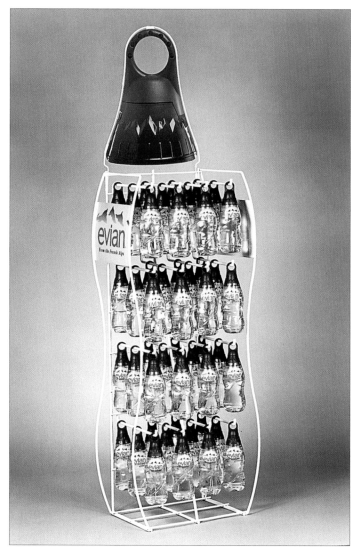

AWARD
Silver

TITLE
Evian Nomad Rack

CLIENT
Danone Waters of North America

ENTRANT
Display Technologies
College Point, New York

SUB-CATEGORY
Soft Drinks, Mineral Water,
and Powdered Mixes

DIVISION
Permanent

AWARD
Silver

TITLE
Dew Domination Clock

CLIENT
Pepsi Cola Company

ENTRANT
The Display Connection
Moonachie, New Jersey

SUB-CATEGORY
Soft Drinks, Mineral Water,
and Powdered Mixes

DIVISION
Permanent

AWARD
Silver

TITLE
Oscar Mayer Lunchables
Fun Snacks Floorstand

CLIENT
Madden Communications

ENTRANT
Trans World Marketing
East Rutherford, New Jersey

SUB-CATEGORY
Snacks, Cookies, and Crackers

DIVISION
Permanent

Snack Products and Soft Drinks

AWARD
Bronze

TITLE
Independent Convenience
Counter Display

CLIENT
Adams Canada

ENTRANT
Adams Canada
(Pfizer Canada, Inc.)
Toronto, Ontario, Canada

SUB-CATEGORY
Candy, Gum, and Mints

DIVISION
Permanent

AWARD
Bronze

TITLE
Kellogg's Single Serve
Mini Power Tower

CLIENT
Kellogg's Company

ENTRANT
Frank Mayer & Associates, Inc.
Grafton, Wisconsin

SUB-CATEGORY
Snacks, Cookies, and Crackers

DIVISION
Permanent

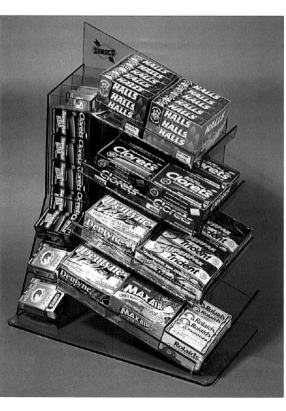

AWARD
Bronze

TITLE
Sunoco Tilt Display

CLIENT
Adams Canada

ENTRANT
Adams Canada
(Pfizer Canada, Inc.)
Toronto, Ontario, Canada

SUB-CATEGORY
Candy, Gum, and Mints

DIVISION
Permanent

AWARD
Bronze

TITLE
Frito-Lay Quick Fit Merchandising System

CLIENT
Frito-Lay USA

ENTRANT
Leggett & Platt Incorporated
Atlanta, Georgia

SUB-CATEGORY
Snacks, Cookies, and Crackers

DIVISION
Permanent

AWARD
Bronze

TITLE
Pepsi/Frito-Lay Millennium Merchandiser

CLIENT
Pepsi Co., Inc

ENTRANT
New Dimensions Research Corp.
Melville, New York

SUB-CATEGORY
Soft Drinks, Mineral Water, and
Powdered Mixes

DIVISION
Permanent

Snack Products and Soft Drinks

AWARD
Gold

TITLE
Coca-Cola Light Book Display

CLIENT
Coca-Cola Nordic AS

ENTRANT
Leo Burnett Oslo
Oslo, Norway

SUB-CATEGORY
Soft Drinks, Mineral Water, and
Powdered Mixes

DIVISION
Semi-Permanent

AWARD
Silver

TITLE
Keebler/Sesame Street
Merchandising Program

CLIENT
Keebler Company

ENTRANT
Packaging Corporation
of America (PCA)
Ashland, Ohio

SUB-CATEGORY
Snacks, Cookies, and Crackers

DIVISION
Semi-Permanent

Snack Products and Soft Drinks

AWARD
Silver

TITLE
Nabisco Truckload Event

CLIENT
Nabisco Ltd.

ENTRANT
Protagon Display, Inc.
Scarborough, Ontario, Canada

SUB-CATEGORY
Snacks, Cookies, and Crackers

DIVISION
Temporary

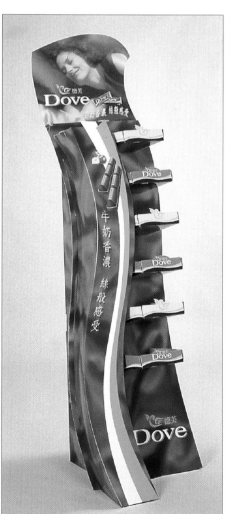

AWARD
Bronze

TITLE
Dove Floor Display

CLIENT
Effem Foods Inc., Taiwan Branch

ENTRANT
AimAsia Integrated Marketing
Network Ltd.
Taipei, Taiwan, R.O.C.

SUB-CATEGORY
Candy, Gum, and Mints

DIVISION
Temporary

AWARD
Bronze

TITLE
Pepsi Choose Your Music
Listening Station

CLIENT
Pepsi Cola Company

ENTRANT
The Display Connection
Moonachie, New Jersey

SUB-CATEGORY
Soft Drinks, Mineral Water,
and Powdered Mixes

DIVISION
Temporary

AWARD
Gold

TITLE
Wilson Golf Smartcore Display System

CLIENT
Wilson Sporting Goods

ENTRANT
Cormark
Elk Grove Village, Illinois

SUB-CATEGORY
Sports Equipment

DIVISION
Permanent

AWARD
Gold

TITLE
LeapFrog Interactive Kiosk

CLIENT
LeapFrog

ENTRANT
Design Phase, Inc.
Northbrook, Illinois

SUB-CATEGORY
Toys

DIVISION
Permanent

Sports, Toys and Accessories

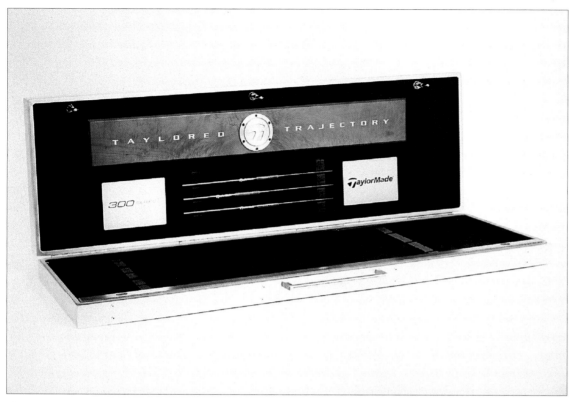

AWARD
Gold

TITLE
Metal Woods Sales Case

CLIENT
NIR Incorporated

ENTRANT
NIR Incorporated and Elge Designs
Portland, Oregon

SUB-CATEGORY
Sports Equipment

DIVISION
Permanent

AWARD
Silver

TITLE
Wilson /Demarini Baseball
Bat Display

CLIENT
Wilson Sporting Goods

ENTRANT
Cormark
Elk Grove Village, Illinois

SUB-CATEGORY
Sports Equipment

DIVISION
Permanent

AWARD
Silver

TITLE
Etonic Virtual Inventory Tower

CLIENT
Spalding Sports Worldwide

ENTRANT
New Dimensions Research Corp.
Melville, New York

SUB-CATEGORY
Sports Equipment

DIVISION
Permanent

AWARD
Silver

TITLE
Interlok News Display

CLIENT
The Washington Post/
The Dallas Morning News

ENTRANT
Santa Cruz Industries and
Franklin Wire Works
Santa Cruz, California

SUB-CATEGORY
Books, Newspapers, and Magazines

DIVISION
Permanent

AWARD
Bronze

TITLE
Wilson Ball Glorifiers

CLIENT
Wilson Sporting Goods

ENTRANT
Cormark
Elk Grove Village, Illinois

SUB-CATEGORY
Sports Equipment

DIVISION
Permanent

AWARD
Bronze

TITLE
Specialized Bike Helmet and Shoe Display

CLIENT
Specialized Bicycle Components

ENTRANT
DCI Marketing
Milwaukee, Wisconsin

SUB-CATEGORY
Sports Equipment

DIVISION
Permanent

AWARD
Bronze

TITLE
LeapFrog LeapPad 5-Wide
Book Display

CLIENT
LeapFrog

ENTRANT
Design Phase, Inc.
Northbrook, Illinois

SUB-CATEGORY
Toys

DIVISION
Permanent

AWARD
Bronze

TITLE
Rapala Store Within A Store

CLIENT
Normark Corporation

ENTRANT
Gage In-Store Marketing
Minneapolis, Minnesota

SUB-CATEGORY
Sports Equipment

DIVISION
Permanent

Sports, Toys and Accessories

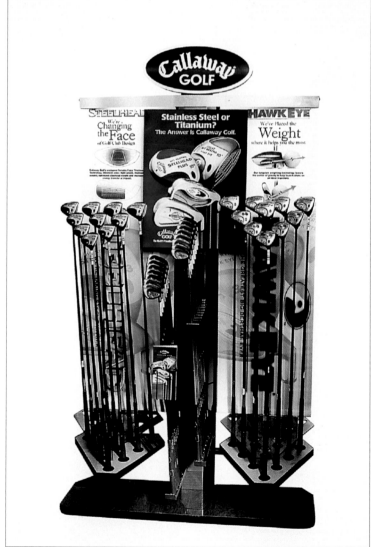

AWARD
Bronze

TITLE
Metal Woods Display

CLIENT
NIR Incorporated

ENTRANT
NIR Incorporated
Portland, Oregon

SUB-CATEGORY
Sports Equipment

DIVISION
Permanent

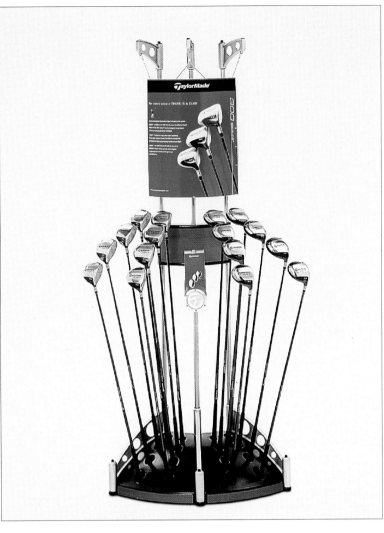

AWARD
Bronze

TITLE
Planet VTech Toys R US Installation

CLIENT
VTech Industries, LLC

ENTRANT
United Displaycraft
Des Plaines, Illinois

SUB-CATEGORY
Toys

DIVISION
Permanent

AWARD
Silver

TITLE
LEGO Star Wars Model Case

CLIENT
LEGO Systems, Inc.

ENTRANT
Frank Mayer & Associates, Inc.
Grafton, Wisconsin

SUB-CATEGORY
Toys

DIVISION
Semi-Permanent

AWARD
Silver

TITLE
Salomon Pilot Floorstand

CLIENT
Salomon North America

ENTRANT
Trans World Marketing
East Rutherford, New Jersey

SUB-CATEGORY
Sports Equipment

DIVISION
Semi-Permanent

AWARD
Bronze

TITLE
Alkaline/Bright Choice
1/4 Pallet Display

CLIENT
Panasonic Industrial Co.

ENTRANT
Advertising Display Company
Lyndhurst, New Jersey

SUB-CATEGORY
Film and Batteries

DIVISION
Semi-Permanent

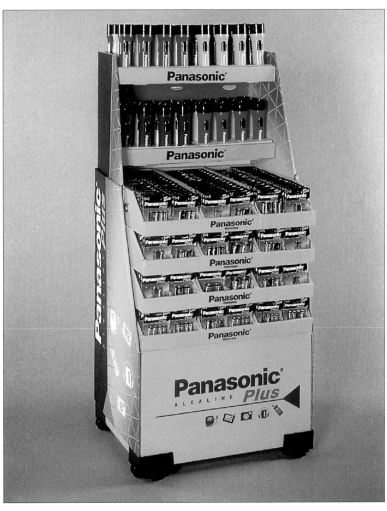

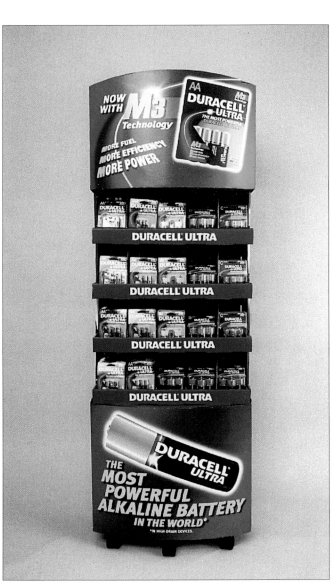

AWARD
Bronze

TITLE
Duracell Rolling Display 2000 for K-Mart

CLIENT
Duracell

ENTRANT
Chesapeake Display & Packaging Co.
Winston-Salem, North Carolina

SUB-CATEGORY
Film and Batteries

DIVISION
Semi-Permanent

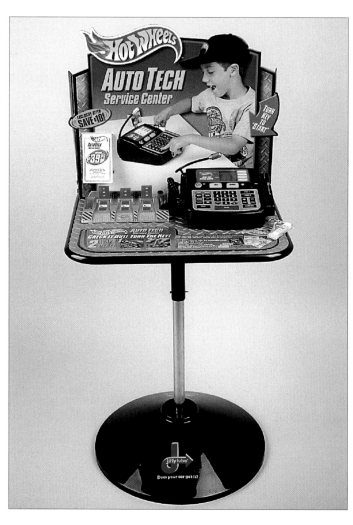

AWARD
Bronze

TITLE
Matte/Jiffy Lube Service Center
Display

CLIENT
Mattel, Inc.

ENTRANT
Cornerstone Display Group Inc.
San Fernando, California

SUB-CATEGORY
Toys

DIVISION
Semi-Permanent

AWARD
Bronze

TITLE
Ranger Rex's Forest Friends Display

CLIENT
RNR, Inc.

ENTRANT
Kell Specialty Products
Chippewa Falls, Wisconsin

SUB-CATEGORY
Toys

DIVISION
Semi-Permanent

AWARD
Bronze

TITLE
Energizer e2 Sidekick

CLIENT
Eveready Battery Company

ENTRANT
Trans World Marketing
East Rutherford, New Jersey

SUB-CATEGORY
Film and Batteries

DIVISION
Semi-Permanent

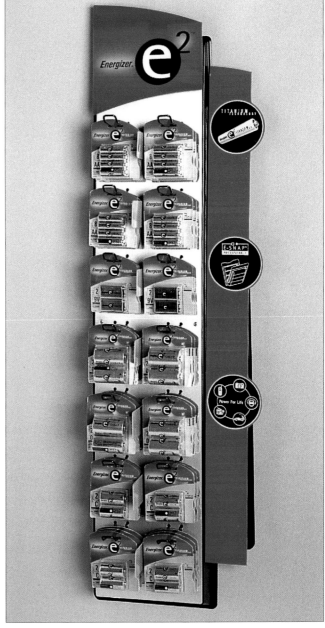

AWARD
Gold

TITLE
Outdoor Products/Wal-Mart BTS Floor
Display

CLIENT
Outdoor Products/Wal-Mart

ENTRANT
Justman Packaging & Display
Los Angeles, California

SUB-CATEGORY
Sports Equipment

DIVISION
Temporary

AWARD
Silver

TITLE
Spalding Rubber Ball Family of Displays

CLIENT
Spalding Sports World Wide

ENTRANT
Henschel-Steinau, Inc.
Englewood, New Jersey

SUB-CATEGORY
Sports Equipment

DIVISION
Temporary

AWARD
Silver

TITLE
DK Essential Computer Floorstand

CLIENT
D.K. Publishing

ENTRANT
Taurus Display Corporation
Cherry Hill, New Jersey

SUB-CATEGORY
Books, Newspapers, and Magazines

DIVISION
Temporary

AWARD
Silver

TITLE
Soccer Floor Display

CLIENT
Lego Systems, Inc.

ENTRANT
Triangle Display Group
Philadelphia, Pennsylvania

SUB-CATEGORY
Toys

DIVISION
Temporary

AWARD
Bronze

TITLE
Angelina Ballerina Floorstand

CLIENT
Pleasant Company

ENTRANT
Great Northern Corporation-Display
Group
Racine, Wisconsin

SUB-CATEGORY
Books, Newspapers, and Magazines

DIVISION
Temporary

Sports, Toys and Accessories

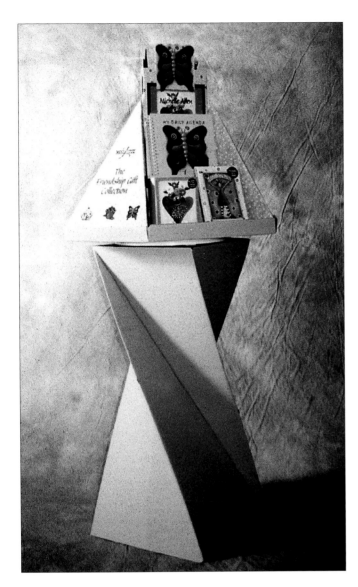

AWARD
Bronze

TITLE
The Friendship Gift Collection

CLIENT
J. Countryman

ENTRANT
LINPAC Displays, Inc.
Tullahoma, Tennessee

SUB-CATEGORY
Books, Newspapers, and Magazines

DIVISION
Temporary

AWARD
Bronze

TITLE
DK K.I.S.S. Floorstand

CLIENT
D.K. Publishing

ENTRANT
Taurus Display Corporation
Cherry Hill, New Jersey

SUB-CATEGORY
Books, Newspapers, and Magazines

DIVISION
Temporary

AWARD
Bronze

TITLE
Titleist 24Dz. Tour Distance SF
Intro Display

CLIENT
Acushnet Company

ENTRANT
Triangle Display Group
Philadelphia, Pennsylvania

SUB-CATEGORY
Sports Equipment

DIVISION
Temporary

AWARD
Bronze

TITLE
Star Wars Floor Display

CLIENT
LEGO Systems, Inc.

ENTRANT
Triangle Display Group
Philadelphia, Pennsylvania

SUB-CATEGORY
Toys

DIVISION
Temporary

AWARD
Bronze

TITLE
The Old Farmer's Almanac 30/8
Floorstand

CLIENT
Yankee Publishing, Inc.

ENTRANT
Triangle Display Group
Philadelphia, Pennsylvania

SUB-CATEGORY
Books, Newspapers, and Magazines

DIVISION
Temporary

Stationery, Office Supplies and Seasonal Goods

AWARD
Gold

TITLE
Target In Line Greeting Card Fixture

CLIENT
American Greetings

ENTRANT
American Greetings Company and United Display
Cleveland, Ohio

SUB-CATEGORY
Greeting Cards

DIVISION
Permanent

AWARD
Silver

TITLE
Bakery Party Cart

CLIENT
American Greetings

ENTRANT
American Greetings Company
and United Display
Cleveland, Ohio

SUB-CATEGORY
Stationary, Party Goods, Gift Wrap, Disposable
Writing Instruments, and Seasonal Goods

DIVISION
Permanent

AWARD
Bronze

TITLE
Milky Product Display & Merchandiser

CLIENT
Pentel of America, Ltd.

ENTRANT
Packaging Corporation of America (PCA)
Burlington, Wisconsin

SUB-CATEGORY
Office Equipment and Supplies

DIVISION
Semi-Permanent

AWARD
Bronze

TITLE
Christmas Pallet

CLIENT
Golden Books Publishing

ENTRANT
Smurfit-Stone Display Group
Carol Stream, Illinois

SUB-CATEGORY
Stationary, Party Goods, Gift Wrap,
Disposable Writing Instruments,
and Seasonal Goods

DIVISION
Temporary

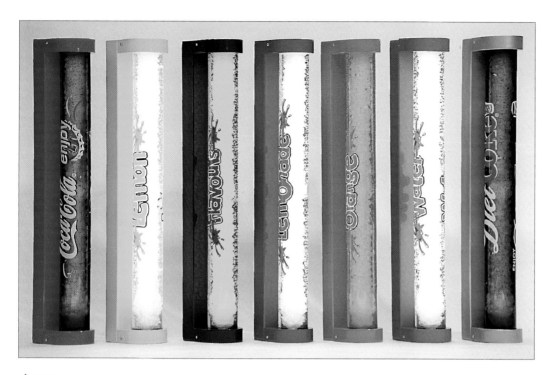

AWARD
Silver

TITLE
Aisle Activation Bubbling Unit Display

CLIENT
Coca-Cola South Pacific

ENTRANT
Airform International Limited
Christchurch, Canterbury, New Zealand

SUB-CATEGORY
Supermarket Retailer
(EDLP/HiLo, Store Size)

DIVISION
Permanent

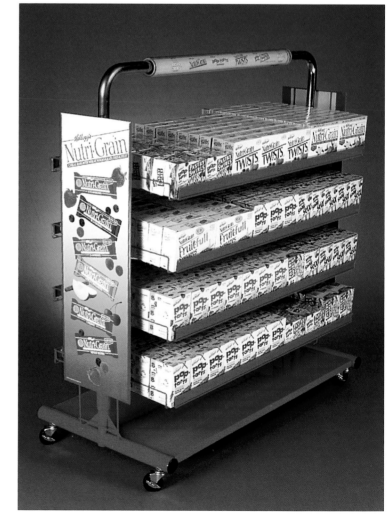

AWARD
Bronze

TITLE
Bruno's End Aisle Merchandiser

CLIENT
Kellogg's Company

ENTRANT
Visual Marketing, Inc.
Chicago, Illinois

SUB-CATEGORY
Supermarket Retailer
(EDLP/HiLo, Store Size)

DIVISION
Permanent

AWARD
Gold

TITLE
"Just The Hits"

CLIENT
Metacom Music

ENTRANT
Meyers Display
Minneapolis, Minnesota

SUB-CATEGORY
Supermarket Retailer
(EDLP/HiLo, Store Size)

DIVISION
Semi-Permanent

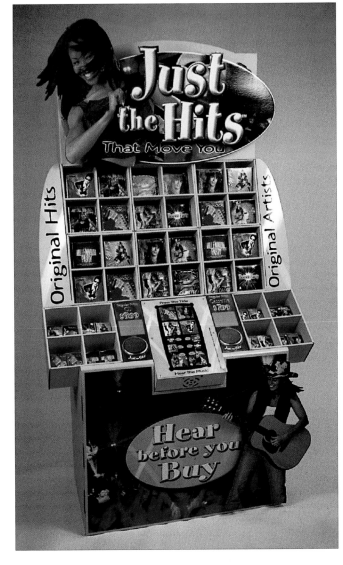

AWARD
Gold

TITLE
H.E.B. Back To School Bus Display

CLIENT
H.E. Butt Grocery

ENTRANT
AG Industries, Inc.
Cleveland, Ohio

SUB-CATEGORY
Supermarket Retailer
(EDLP/HiLo, Store Size)

DIVISION
Temporary

Supermarket Retailer

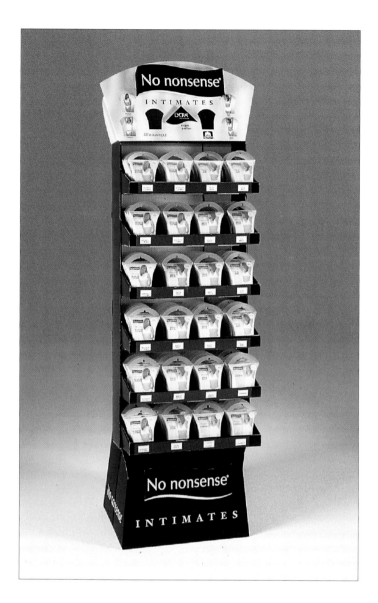

AWARD
Silver

TITLE
No Nonsense Intimates
Floor Display

CLIENT
New York Phenomenon, Ltd.

ENTRANT
Triangle Display Group
Philadelphia, Pennsylvania

SUB-CATEGORY
Supermarket Retailer
(EDLP/HiLo, Store Size)

DIVISION
Temporary

AWARD
Bronze

TITLE
2 in 1 Floor Display/ Power Wing

CLIENT
Colgate Palmolive Company

ENTRANT
Henschel-Steinau, Inc.
Englewood, New Jersey

SUB-CATEGORY
Supermarket Retailer
(EDLP/HiLo, Store Size)

DIVISION
Temporary

AWARD
Silver

TITLE
Bailey's-Cigarette 2 Tier Counter Display

CLIENT
S & M Brands, Inc.

ENTRANT
Nashville Display Manufacturing Co.
Nashville, Tennessee

SUB-CATEGORY
Cigarettes – Non-Illuminated

DIVISION
Permanent

AWARD
Bronze

TITLE
Salem Gravity Feed Counter Display

CLIENT
R. J. Reynolds Tobacco Company

ENTRANT
ImageWorks Display & Marketing Group, Inc.
Winston-Salem, North Carolina

SUB-CATEGORY
Cigarettes – Non-Illuminated

DIVISION
Permanent

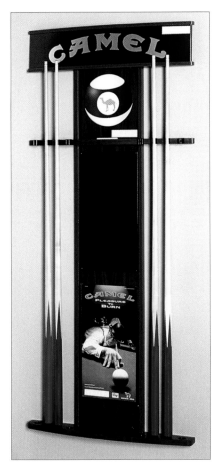

AWARD
Bronze

TITLE
Camel Pool Cue Rack

CLIENT
R. J. Reynolds Tobacco Company

ENTRANT
Trans World Marketing
East Rutherford, New Jersey

SUB-CATEGORY
Cigarettes – Non-Illuminated

DIVISION
Permanent

AWARD
Gold

TITLE
Doral Jam Packed B2G1F

CLIENT
R. J. Reynolds Tobacco Company

ENTRANT
Chesapeake Display & Packaging Co.
Winston-Salem, North Carolina

SUB-CATEGORY
Cigarettes – Non-Illuminated

DIVISION
Semi-Permanent

AWARD
Silver

TITLE
Winston B2G2F Counter Display

CLIENT
R. J. Reynolds Tobacco Company

ENTRANT
Chesapeake Display & Packaging Co.
Winston-Salem, North Carolina

SUB-CATEGORY
Cigarettes – Non-Illuminated

DIVISION
Semi-Permanent

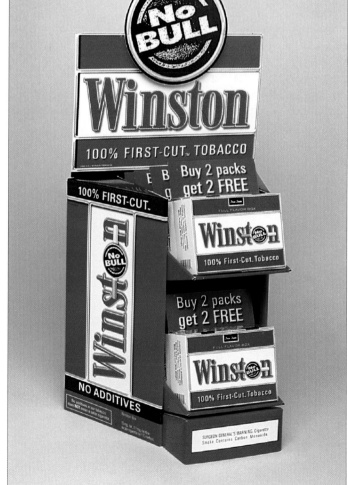

AWARD
Bronze

TITLE
Salem Global Menthol Display

CLIENT
R. J. Reynolds Tobacco Company

ENTRANT
Chesapeake Display & Packaging Co.
Winston-Salem, North Carolina

SUB-CATEGORY
Cigarettes – Non-Illuminated

DIVISION
Semi-Permanent

AWARD
Bronze

TITLE
Doral Jam Box CTS Floor Display

CLIENT
R. J. Reynolds Tobacco Company

ENTRANT
CorrFlex Display & Packaging
Statesville, North Carolina

SUB-CATEGORY
Cigarettes – Non-Illuminated

DIVISION
Semi-Permanent

Tobacco

AWARD
Gold

TITLE
Camel Turkish Gold New Product Launch

CLIENT
R. J. Reynolds Tobacco Company

ENTRANT
CorrFlex Display & Packaging
Statesville, North Carolina

SUB-CATEGORY
Cigarettes – Non-Illuminated

DIVISION
Temporary

AWARD
Silver

TITLE
Camel 57 Chevy MultiPack Offer Ctop

CLIENT
R. J. Reynolds Tobacco Company

ENTRANT
CorrFlex Display & Packaging
Statesville, North Carolina

SUB-CATEGORY
Cigarettes – Non-Illuminated

DIVISION
Temporary

AWARD
Bronze

TITLE
Camel B2G1 Pleasure to Burn
Counter Promotion

CLIENT
R. J. Reynolds Tobacco Company

ENTRANT
CorrFlex Display & Packaging
Statesville, North Carolina

SUB-CATEGORY
Cigarettes – Non-Illuminated

DIVISION
Temporary

AWARD
Gold

TITLE
Harley-Davidson Seat Demonstrator

CLIENT
Harley-Davidson

ENTRANT
DCI Marketing
Milwaukee, Wisconsin

SUB-CATEGORY
Automotive Aftermarket

DIVISION
Permanent

AWARD
Silver

TITLE
Ford Accessory Merchandiser

CLIENT
Ford Motor Company

ENTRANT
DCI Marketing
Milwaukee, Wisconsin

SUB-CATEGORY
Passenger Cars and Specialty Vehicles

DIVISION
Permanent

Transportation

AWARD
Silver

TITLE
F Series/Econoline Mktg Materials Tool Box

CLIENT
Marketing Associates

ENTRANT
Westcott Displays, Inc.
Detroit, Michigan

SUB-CATEGORY
Petroleum Products

DIVISION
Permanent

AWARD
Bronze

TITLE
Harley-Davidson Tire
and Rim Fixture

CLIENT
Harley-Davidson

ENTRANT
DCI Marketing
Milwaukee, Wisconsin

SUB-CATEGORY
Automotive Aftermarket

DIVISION
Permanent

AWARD
Bronze

TITLE
Toyota Key Accessory Products Display

CLIENT
Toyota Motor Sales U.S.A., Inc.

ENTRANT
Innovative Marketing Solutions, Inc.
Bensenville, Illinois

SUB-CATEGORY
Automotive Aftermarket

DIVISION
Permanent

AWARD
Bronze

TITLE
Acura Full Size Rear Spoiler

CLIENT
American Honda Motor Co., Inc.

ENTRANT
Santa Cruz Industries
Santa Cruz, California

SUB-CATEGORY
Passenger Cars and Specialty Vehicles

DIVISION
Permanent

Transportation

AWARD
Silver

TITLE
Dodge Stratus/Caravan
Launch Display

CLIENT
InterOne Marketing

ENTRANT
Westcott Displays, Inc.
Detroit, Michigan

SUB-CATEGORY
Passenger Cars and Specialty Vehicles

DIVISION
Semi-Permanent

AWARD
Bronze

TITLE
Fram Floor Display

CLIENT
Honeywell, Inc.

ENTRANT
Taurus Display Corporation
Cherry Hill, New Jersey

SUB-CATEGORY
Petroleum Products

DIVISION
Temporary

Multinational
Awards Contest

The Multinational Contest recognizes the merchandising excellence of displays produced and placed outside the United States, Europe and Japan.

AWARD
Gold

TITLE
Time Force Display Program

CLIENT
Time Force Mexico S.A. de C.V.

ENTRANT
APTO Frank Mayer
Lomas de Bezares, DF, Mexico

SUB-CATEGORY
Multinational Contest

DIVISION
Permanent

AWARD
Silver

TITLE
Coors Light Vortex Neon

CLIENT
Integer Group/Coors

ENTRANT
Everbrite, Inc.
Greenfield, Wisconsin

SUB-CATEGORY
Multinational Contest

DIVISION
Permanent

AWARD
Bronze

TITLE
Sears Mini-Stack

CLIENT
Sears Canada

ENTRANT
CDA Industries, Inc.
Pickering, Ontario, Canada

SUB-CATEGORY
Multinational Contest

DIVISION
Permanent

AWARD
Bronze

TITLE
Angel Face Self Standing Display

CLIENT
Unilever Mexico (Pond's), S.A. de C.V.

ENTRANT
Armo Diseno, POP, S.C.
Mexico, DF, Mexico

SUB-CATEGORY
Multinational Contest

DIVISION
Permanent

AWARD
Bronze

TITLE
Azaléia Moldura Display

CLIENT
Calçados Azaléia S/A

ENTRANT
M.A./Frank Mayer
Porto Alegre, Brazil

SUB-CATEGORY
Multinational Contest

DIVISION
Permanent

Multinational

AWARD
Gold

TITLE
Cappuccino Self Standing Display

CLIENT
Nestlé México, S.A. de C.V.

ENTRANT
Armo Diseno, POP, S.C.
Mexico DF, Mexico

SUB-CATEGORY
Multinational Contest

DIVISION
Semi-Permanent

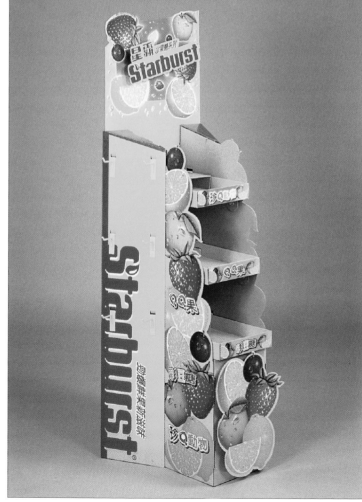

AWARD
Bronze

TITLE
Starburst Floor Display

CLIENT
Effem Foods Inc., Taiwan Branch

ENTRANT
AimAsia Integrated Marketing Network Ltd.
Taipei, Taiwan, R.O.C.

SUB-CATEGORY
Multinational Contest

DIVISION
Semi-Permanent

AWARD
Bronze

TITLE
Olympikus Spider Display

CLIENT
Calçados Azaléia S/A

ENTRANT
M.A./Frank Mayer
Porto Alegre, Brazil

SUB-CATEGORY
Multinational Contest

DIVISION
Semi-Permanent

AWARD
Bronze

TITLE
Plano For Samsung (New Point)

CLIENT
Samsung Electronics Co., Ltd.

ENTRANT
POP BANK Co., Ltd.
Seoul, Korea

SUB-CATEGORY
Multinational Contest

DIVISION
Semi-Permanent

AWARD
Silver

TITLE
Kit Kat Chunky Floor Stands & Counter Unit

CLIENT
Nestle Australia Limited

ENTRANT
Ace Print & Display Pty Ltd.
Revesby, NSW, Australia

SUB-CATEGORY
Multinational Contest

DIVISION
Temporary

AWARD
Silver

TITLE
M & M's Crispy Display

CLIENT
Mars Confectionery of Australia

ENTRANT
Visy Displays
(A Division of Pratt Industries)
Reservoir, Victoria, Australia

SUB-CATEGORY
Multinational Contest

DIVISION
Temporary

AWARD
Bronze

TITLE
Haze Hangstell Unit

CLIENT
Reckitt Benkiser

ENTRANT
ACB Packaging and Displays
Sydney, N.S.W, Australia

SUB-CATEGORY
Multinational Contest

DIVISION
Temporary

AWARD
Bronze

TITLE
Revlon Foiled Passion Floor Display

CLIENT
Revlon Taiwan Co., Ltd.

ENTRANT
AimAsia Integrated Marketing
Network Ltd.
Taipei, Taiwan, R.O.C.

SUB-CATEGORY
Multinational Contest

DIVISION
Temporary

AWARD
Bronze

TITLE
L'Oréal Quick Stick Floor Display

CLIENT
L'Oréal
Taiwan Co., Ltd.

ENTRANT
AimAsia Integrated Marketing Network Ltd.
Taipei, Taiwan, R.O.C.

SUB-CATEGORY
Multinational Contest

DIVISION
Temporary

Technical Awards Contest

POPAI's Technical Awards recognizeengineering excellence and the innovative use of materials in P-O-P design.

AWARD
Gold

TITLE
Aisle Activation Bubbling Unit Display

CLIENT
Coca-Cola South Pacific

ENTRANT
Airform International Limited
Christchurch, Canterbury, New Zealand

SUB-CATEGORY
Supermarket Retailer (EDLP/HiLo, Store Size)

DIVISION
Permanent

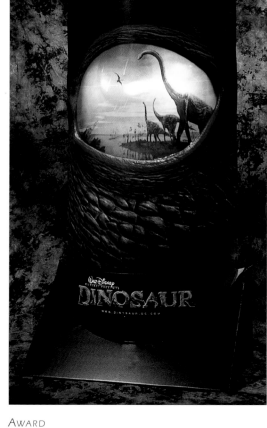

AWARD
Gold

TITLE
Illuminated Dinosaur Standee

CLIENT
Walt Disney Studios

ENTRANT
Rapid Displays
Chicago, Illinois

SUB-CATEGORY
Movies, Tapes, Records, CDs

DIVISION
Semi-Permanent

AWARD
Silver

TITLE
Bat Wing Goggles

CLIENT
Reflective Technology

ENTRANT
Accent Display Corporation
Cranston, Rhode Island

SUB-CATEGORY
Apparel and Sewing Notions

DIVISION
Permanent

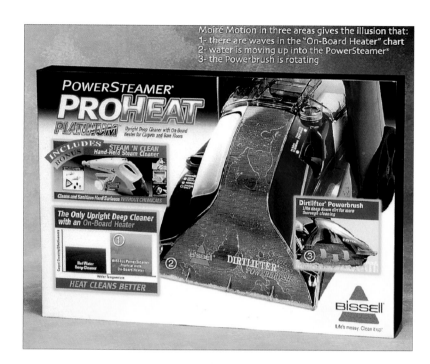

AWARD
Silver

TITLE
Bissell "Proheat" Moire Sign

CLIENT
Bissell

ENTRANT
Rapid Displays
Union City, California

SUB-CATEGORY
Non-Illuminated

DIVISION
Temporary

AWARD
Bronze

TITLE
Interactive Memory Game Trakinas

CLIENT
Fleischman Royal Nabisco

ENTRANT
Droid Tecnologia Promocional and Art Contrast
São Paulo SP, Brazil

SUB-CATEGORY
National

DIVISION
Permanent

AWARD
Bronze

TITLE
Matrix® Display Systems
Grinch Photo Blanket

CLIENT
Nabisco Inc.

ENTRANT
3 Strikes Custom Design
Stamford, Connecticut

SUB-CATEGORY
Regional

DIVISION
Temporary

Index of Displays